D1296391

Father, Son,
and Healing Ghosts

Anthony T. Moore

Center for Applications of Psychological Type, Inc.
Gainesville, Florida

Published by the Center for Applications of Psychological Type, Inc.
2815 NW 13th Street
Suite 401
Gainesville, Florida 32609
(352)375-0160

ISBN 0-935652-52-3

Library of Congress Cataloging-in-Publication Data

Moore, Anthony T., 1944–
     Father, son, and healing ghosts / by Anthony T. Moore.
          p. cm.
     Includes bibliographical references.
     ISBN 0-935652-52-3
      1. Jungian psychology. 2. Psychoanalysis. 3. Loss (Psychology) 4. Fathers and sons. 5. Self actualization (Psychology) 6. Moore, Anthony T., 1944– I. Title.

     BF175 .M634 2000
     150.19'54–dc21   00–023243

Acknowledgements

I gratefully acknowledge the use of the following materials:

"Digging" from *Opened Ground: Selected Poems 1966-1996* by Seamus Heaney. © 1998 by Seamus Heaney. Reprinted by permission of Farrar, Straus and Giroux, LLC, and Faber and Faber.

"In Memorial" from *Marine Verses from WW II* by Carl Dearborn.

Selections from *The Aeneid* by Virgil. Translated by C. H. Sisson. © 1986 by Carcanet Press. Reprinted by permission of Carcanet Press.

Selections from *Ego and Archetype* by Edward F. Edinger. © 1972 by the C.G. Jung Foundation for Analytical Psychology. Reprinted by permission of Shambhala Publications, Inc.

Selections from *Inner Work* by Robert A. Johnson. © 1986 by Robert A. Johnson. Reprinted by permission of HarperCollins Publishers, Inc.

Selections from *Letters. Vol. 1. 1906-1950* by C. G. Jung. © 1973 by Princeton University Press. Reprinted by permission of Princeton University Press.

Selections from *The Making of a Mind* by Pierre Teilhard de Chardin. Originally published in French as *Genese d'Une Pensee.* © 1961 by Editions Bernard Grasset. English Edition 1965 by Harper & Row. Reprinted by permission of Georges Borchardt, Inc.

Selections from *Memories, Dreams, Reflections* by C. G. Jung. Recorded and edited by Aniela Jaffe. © 1965 by Vintage Books. Reprinted by permission of Pantheon Books, a Division of Random House.

Selections from *The Spiritual Exercises of St. Ignatius.* Translated by Louis J. Puhl, S.J. © 1951 by Newman Press. Reprinted by permission of Loyola University Press.

Selections from "Christmas Eve on Maui" by Charles A. Landmesser. *Leatherneck: Magazine of the Marines,* December, 1949.

Selections from *A Personal Account of World War II* by Albert Arsenault.

Selections from the following volumes of C. G. Jung's *Collected Works* are reprinted by permission of Princeton University Press:

Volume 5 *Symbols of Transformation*.
© 1956 by Bollingen Foundation, Inc.

Volume 9, Part I *The Archetypes and the Collective Unconscious*.
© 1959 by Bollingen Foundation, Inc.
New Material © 1969 by Princeton University Press.

Volume 9, Part II *Aion*.
© 1959 by Bollingen Foundation, Inc.

Volume 10 *Civilization in Transition*.
© 1964 by Bollingen Foundation, Inc.
Second Edition © 1970 by Princeton University Press.

Volume 11 *Psychology and Religion: West and East*.
© 1958 by Bollingen Foundation, Inc.
Second Edition © 1969 by Princeton University Press.

Volume 12 *Psychology and Alchemy*.
© 1953 by Bollingen Foundation, Inc.
New Material © 1968 by Bollingen Foundation, Inc.

Volume 13 *Alchemical Studies*.
© 1967 by Bollingen Foundation, Inc.

Volume 14 *Mysterium Coniunctionis*.
© 1963 by Bollingen Foundation, Inc.
Second Edition © 1970 by Princeton University Press.

Volume 18 *The Symbolic Life*.
© 1976 by Princeton University Press.

I wish to thank my editor, Tom Thompson, and the staff of the Center for Applications of Psychological Type, especially Gerald Macdaid and Charles Martin, for making the publication of this book so easy and enjoyable. I am grateful also for the many friends and family members who encouraged me in writing this book. I particularly wish to express my gratitude to my mother whose memory of my father made me want to know him, to the veterans of the Fourth Marine Division of World War II for helping me to find him, and to my wife, Michelle, for being my companion on this journey.

Table of Contents

1 Prelude

1st. Lt. Anthony Thomas Moore
24th Marines, 4th Marine Division
Killed in action
Saipan, Marianas Islands, South Pacific
June 15, 1944

My father was killed the first night the Marines landed on Saipan. I was two months old. He was twenty-three. This is the story of my search for him and, finally, for my self.

I never saw my father and he never saw me, but I do know that he saw pictures of my baptism. My mother told me I threw up the first time she breast-fed me after she received the telegram informing her of his death. But my earliest memory of loss probably goes back to the age of three or four. I had crawled under the dining room table, one of my favorite hiding spots, and I could hear adults talking in the living room. The sad whispers of grown-ups' voices crept into my safe haven. I don't remember exactly what they were talking about. I just recall a deep sense of sadness coming over me, a feeling that somebody special was missing. I must have wanted to avoid this feeling because I also remember that, later on and throughout my childhood, I would usually respond to any inquiries about my father by saying casually, "You can't miss what you never had."

I was raised by my mother and my maternal grandparents. A portrait of my father wearing a Marine dress green uniform sat on my mother's dresser all the years I was growing up, like a sacred icon watching over my childhood. As a kid, I seemed to be fascinated by anything associated with the Marines: uniforms, movies, even the *Marine Corps Hymn*—anything that reminded me of my father. When I had no one else to play with, I would dress up wearing his green garrison cap with a bronze 2nd lieutenant's bar on it. My mother must have carried these precious mementos home with her when my father shipped out for the Pacific and she returned from Laguna Beach, California to live with her parents in Cohoes, New York. I always presumed my father's silver 1st lieutenant's bars were with him when he died.

My fascination with military uniforms carried over into my choice of high schools. I went to a military high school in part to imitate my father's life in uniform. I completely immersed myself in the spit and polish of a cadet's life. I wanted to do it as well as my father, so of course I had to be an officer. At the end of four years, I felt I had had enough of the military, so in college I avoided ROTC. But in my senior year I began thinking again about the Marines. I took the entrance exam for the Marine Corps Officer Candidate School, just as my father had. It was 1966 and the conflict in Vietnam was intensifying. With the enthusiasm and naivete of a twenty-two-year-old, and because I really had nothing better to do, I concluded Vietnam was the place to be because that was where the action would be for my generation. Joining the Marines was also one more way to imitate my father who had enlisted in the spring of his senior year in college, 1942. But when I told my mother and grandmother what I was contemplating, I realized that the similarities to my father's situation, which inspired me, were more than they could handle. As I looked into their eyes, I realized that I could also be killed just as my father had been. I wanted to do something significant with my life, dedicate myself completely to a worthy cause, but I also wanted to live. Since I had an automatic deferment as the sole surviving son of someone killed in action, I moved back home to live with my mother and grandparents and took a job as a management trainee for General Electric while I decided what to do next. A year later, I entered the Novitiate of the Society of Jesus in Poughkeepsie, New York.

Joining the Jesuits felt like the right move for a number of reasons. During my college days at Fordham University, I was impressed by the integrity and intelligence of my Jesuit professors. They presented an image of manhood that I found both intellectually and emotionally inspiring. With their academic credentials and scholarly dedication they became ready father substitutes for a young man looking for role models. Most of them were also Irish like my father. One even looked a little like him with his reddish hair and high forehead. But there was more to my motivation than the imitation of role models.

The priesthood had attracted me as long as I could remember. I can still see myself as a small boy kneeling next to my mother in the choir loft of a Catholic church that had once been a brewery, my face pressed against the dark mahogany bars of the choir railing. Something in the drama being played out below me held my rapt attention. Later, when I learned to follow the Latin Mass in my English missal, I was able to understand the meaning of the ritual and to focus on my own part in the sacred action. One prayer in particular stood out for me because it expressed what I believed to be the most important part of the Mass. It was the prayer for the dead that put into solemn words my own reason for being at Mass:

Memento etiam, Domine, famulorum famularumque tuarum, qui nos praecesserunt cum signo fidei, et dormiunt in somno pacis.

Remember also, O Lord, Thy servants and handmaids who have gone before us with the sign of faith, and rest in the sleep of peace.

Here the rubrics directed me to mention by name any of the dead I wished to remember. As I whispered to myself the words, "my father," I sensed I was somehow with him and he was with me. I could not explain how but it was clear that in the liturgy of the Mass I experienced a unique moment of contact with my father. At Mass I discovered a mystery that transcended the power of death. Being a priest was a way to enter more fully into the power of that mystery.

Joining the Jesuits was also a way of doing something with the same commitment and dedication that led my father to join the Marines, a dedication so complete that it ended in his giving his life: Greater love has no man than this, that a man lay down his life for his friends (John 15:13). I wanted to be worthy of the sacrifice my father had made. I wanted to be the kind of man my father had been. Being a Jesuit was like being a Marine. Sometimes the Jesuits were even referred to as the Pope's Marines. Furthermore, the idea of joining a religious order carried with it an image of dying, dying to the world, particularly the world of marital love. When I entered the Jesuits, I was twenty-three years old. Only years later did I realize that was the same age my father was when he died.

In the Jesuits, I learned a form of meditation that would eventually be helpful in my search for my father. An essential part of Jesuit training is a thirty-day silent retreat based on the *Spiritual Exercises* of St. Ignatius Loyola, the founder of the Jesuits. The *Spiritual Exercises* teach a method of prayer that engages the imagination in an inner dialogue with characters from one's own life and the life of Christ. This method yielded a rich harvest of reflection that initiated a process of inner healing, but it seemed to stall around issues related to my father. A key meditation involves an intimate dialogue with God the Father. Surprisingly, I was unable to develop any real feeling around this conversation except one of frustration. For all my fascination with things pertaining to my father, he remained somehow affectively unreal and emotionally unavailable to me. These spiritual exercises clarified areas of my inner life in which I needed healing and provided a means to begin that healing.

As a Jesuit, I was happy with the life of prayer, service, and community, but the life of celibacy left me feeling empty and alone. I missed the warmth and understanding of close friendships with women. The result was a constant struggle between my desire to be a priest and my longing for female companionship. The conflict was further complicated by my awareness that my father's death followed closely upon my birth and my irrational and barely conscious fear that I too would die if I fathered a child. More importantly, I believed that becoming a priest was a debt I owed my father for the sacrifice he made in giving up his life for me. He never had the opportunity to fully live his life, so I was living for both of us. If I wasted my life on something meaningless, I would be wasting his life and sacrifice as well.

The fact that I carried his name increased this sense of identification. I grew up wearing tie clasps and carrying handkerchiefs that bore his initials and mine. I couldn't do whatever I pleased. I had to live my life in a way that was worthy of being the continuation of his. At the time, being a Jesuit priest seemed to be the best way to fulfill my duty and connect to my father. The loneliness of a celibate life was simply the price I would have to pay to be true to what I believed to be my destiny.

Eventually, my inner conflict and confusion caused so much turmoil that I asked my religious superiors if I could see a psychiatrist. With their permission and financial support, I began three years of psychoanalysis with a female psychiatrist. For the first time I learned how to directly engage the unconscious through analyzing my dreams. This method helped clarify many of the psychological distortions that inhibited my freedom. I realized that I identified with my father so completely that I was unable to be myself. Somehow, I needed to distinguish my own identity from my father's so I could live my own life. My analyst also helped me to see that even at the deepest unconscious level there was something very positive and life-giving about my attraction to the priesthood and that being a priest contributed significantly to healing the loss I felt from my father's death.

With my analyst's help, I also learned to enjoy and cherish my maternal grandfather who raised me and loved me but whose volatility often frightened me. Joe Bochini completed only two years of school in Italy before he went to work on a mule train with his father. At the age of seventeen, he left home for America. It was clear that "Nonnon" was proud of me and his other two grandsons, but his lack of education and unpredictable temper kept me from really accepting him as the surrogate father he so obviously was. Instead, I preferred to pretend that I did not really need a father, that I had learned to be my own father. With my usual rejoinder, I said to my analyst, "You can't miss what you never had." Her answer cut through my denial. She replied, "You can also miss what you never had but know you had every right to have." Once I was able to admit my feelings of loss, I began to realize how much the presence of my Italian grandfather had managed to fill the vacuum.

As I recounted stories about my grandfather, my analyst learned to admire and respect him and she taught me to do likewise. Through my analyst's positive regard and real affection for this difficult old Italian, I was able to accept the powerful role he played in my development as a man. In contrast to my father, my grandfather was very much alive and emotionally very real. Gradually, my grandfather began to work his way into my sense of self. I began to realize just how much this flawed but real man had been there as a father for me. Through the process of psychoanalysis I was finally able to grant him the place in my conscious identity that he always had in my heart. I let him be the father he had always been—three years after his death. Allowing myself to be my grandfather's son loosened the paralyzing grip of my over-identification with my father. By allowing my grandfather to assume a role within my conscious identity, I was able to establish some sense of identity distinct from my father.

Some separation from my father's identity was necessary for me to be free to lead my own life, but once the distinction was established I needed to reconnect to the energy and meaning that continued to flow from the image of my father. My questions about the limitations of celibacy remained, but the experience of psychoanalysis taught me that the idea of priesthood and the search for my father exercised a powerful unifying role in my psyche. So I decided to move forward toward ordination.

In November of 1979, at the age of thirty-five, I was ordained a deacon, the last stage in the process toward priesthood. Lying prostrate in prayer on the sanctuary floor, I could vividly sense my father's presence in the ordination ritual. While the congregation intoned the Litany of Saints invoking the intercession of the saints in heaven on behalf of those being ordained, I felt as though I were enacting a scene that had come to comfort my father as he lay dying on an island in the Pacific. In my imagination, I saw him at the moment of death consoled by a vision of his son's ordination. I had no actual knowledge of his thoughts at the moment of death, but this spontaneous image made my experience of the ordination ritual profoundly meaningful and moving. Some kind of healing was taking place through the symbolic actions that constituted priestly ordination. Although many doubts persisted, I knew I had to move forward to the final stage of priesthood. I had to finish the journey I had begun.

On June 14, 1980, I was ordained a priest. Following a ritual rich in medieval imagery, I placed my joined hands within the palms of the ordaining bishop. Then the bishop anointed my hands with oil and placed his hands on my head. Finally, all the priests present joined the bishop imposing hands on those being ordained. As each of the more than a hundred men touched the top of my head, I could feel the warmth and strength of their fatherly blessings.

The next day, I celebrated my First Mass. On June 15, the 36th anniversary of my father's death, I led my family in prayer: "Remember, Lord, those who have died and have gone before us marked with the sign of faith, especially those for whom we now pray." As I voiced the words of this prayer, I again felt my father's presence. The coincidence of the anniversary of his death with my first ritual action as a priest intensified my feeling of destiny. This was a stage in my journey that I had to complete, but I was soon to learn that my journey was far from over.

Although I believed I was doing what I was destined to do, I did so with a divided heart. By being ordained a priest I was completing a mission entrusted to me at my father's death, but I was also aware of a longing deep in my soul that remained unfulfilled. I felt a hole inside of me which, no matter how hard I tried, I could not fill. It was a deep, pervasive longing that would not let me go, as though something were missing at the core of my being and needed to be found.

Ordination marked a significant and necessary moment of healing, but the process of healing was far from complete. Although I did not understand it at the time, I now see that through the sacred rituals of ordination and First Mass, I had somehow connected to my father's *spirit*. Once that phase of my healing reached its natural term, the longing of my heart began leading me in a way that would connect me to my father's *humanity*.

One of the most valuable things I learned from the experience of psychoanalysis was that psychic healing requires the ability to feel pain. Now I was about to learn that a close loving relationship was the only thing that could provide the kind of environment in which I felt safe enough to feel the pain that lay deep within my unconscious.

I had a number of close friends over the sixteen years that I was a Jesuit, but there was one particular person and one particular moment that marked a turning point in my experience with relationships. Michelle and I had been friends for a couple of years when I asked her if she would like to take a ride with me. Without really understanding why, I suggested we drive to the Catskill Mountains of New York State. My father's family came from that area. Some of his nieces and nephews still lived there, but my purpose in going there was not to visit them. I just had a feeling I needed to be in those mountains and I wanted to share them with this friend.

Since we had no specific destination, we drove casually through the mountains enjoying each other's company and the rolling countryside. Almost without thinking about it, I found myself driving to the farm where my father grew up. One of my cousins now owned the farm, but I was embarrassed to stop by unannounced. Instead, we stopped at a hay field along the highway half a mile from the farmhouse. As Michelle and I walked through the field, I recounted to her memories of working in this field with my father's brother and his sons. I could see myself as a small boy straining to throw the hay bales onto a wagon. I also recalled my mother telling me that my father proposed to her in this field under the light of an August moon.

We walked around the field and returned to the car. Again without quite realizing why, I found myself driving up the hill that led to the cemetery where my father lay buried between his parents and his favorite sister, Rita. As a child I had often visited my father's grave with my mother and grandmother. This was the first time I ever brought a friend. Michelle and I stood quietly before my father's tombstone and said a prayer.

Then, instead of driving back down to the main road, I continued driving farther up the mountain along a road I had never taken before. As I drove, I started to feel a deep sadness welling up inside of me. I felt so bad that I had to stop the car. I got out and walked into an open field. Down below I could see the house where my grandmother lived after she moved off the farm. Michelle followed me into the field. As I turned and put an arm around her, I began to cry, a deep convulsive crying that seemed to well up from the hidden recesses of my being. The sadness of a little boy who has lost his father came rushing into my awareness. Never before had I allowed myself to feel this much pain. Finally, I was letting myself feel the pain I had avoided and denied for so many years. Because Michelle was there and because I trusted her, I was able to let myself experience the emptiness that I had carried in my heart as long as I could remember. It was as though I had touched the bottom of a pit and now the hole could be filled. Never again did the hole feel as though it could not be filled. Because I was no longer denying some of the pain, a deeper level of healing became possible.

Because I was able to allow myself to feel my pain in the presence of Michelle, I knew that she held the key that would help me to open the deeper recesses of my heart. If I could trust her with this, I could trust her with anything. From that moment, I realized that I had to redirect my life in such a way that she could become a permanent part of it. This journey to my father's grave was a significant factor in my decision to leave the Jesuits and marry Michelle. In Michelle's presence, I felt secure enough to experience and share the pain of my father's loss and thus continue the healing that began with my psychoanalysis.

Three years after my ordination, I left the Jesuits and married Michelle. By the time I was forty, I had a wife, two stepsons, a home, a mortgage, and a new career. I thought I had successfully weathered my mid-life crisis and was ready to settle in for a life of relative psychological stability. With the customary concerns and anxieties of a new husband and father in the forefront of my awareness, the quest for my father moved to a back burner.

It was therefore somewhat of a shock when, several years later, I viewed the movie *Field of Dreams* for the first time. As the end of the movie drew near I had a sense that something powerful was about to happen to me. As Ray Kinsella looked at the last player remaining on his magical baseball field, I could feel something rising up inside of me. It was a sense of possibilities, the possibility that Ray was about to see once more his father who had died years previously. Somehow that possibility merged with the possibility, the hope, that I might someday finally meet my father, a hope that lay buried within me for as long as I could remember.

When Ray recognized his father and they shook hands, something let go inside of me. It was as though I were experiencing what it would feel like to actually stand face to face with my father. The tears came welling up from somewhere deep inside, but there was a strange sense of satisfaction in their flowing warmly and freely over my cheeks. It was no longer just the feeling of emptiness, but of a longing somehow fulfilled, of a hope somehow realized. The feeling was so strong, so satisfying, while at the same time perplexing and aching, that I did something I had never done before. I was watching the movie on videocassette, and when it was over I rewound the tape and watched the whole movie all over again—again, the same powerful emotional reaction.

I was aware that this movie touched something deep, almost primordial, inside of me, but I was not sure how. I was intrigued by how it could move me so deeply. I had been affected by similar movies before, but not at the same level. Was there something special about this movie that made it happen or was it just something that was happening inside of me? I wasn't sure what to do, but I thought the questions were worthy of attention so I just let them sit in the back of my mind. I knew they would come forward when they needed to be addressed.

In the weeks that followed an odd process gradually began to take shape. As I was in the shower with the water running down over me, an image from the movie would drop into my consciousness. Then, right alongside the movie image, a piece of Carl Jung's theory would drop into place. I had been teaching Jungian psychology for several years and had found his categories relevant in understanding my own spiritual and psychological development and in helping other people with their developmental issues. Only later did I realize that Jung had actually referred to the kind of experience I was having with his theory and this movie. He wrote, "We can really produce precious little by our conscious mind. All the time we are dependent upon the things that fall into our consciousness; therefore in German we call them *Einfalle* (ideas)."[1] These ideas and images were falling into my consciousness just as Jung described. At the time, I wasn't sure what to make of it.

I shared my spontaneous thoughts with my wife. After the third or fourth morning of interrupting her coffee with some observation about the similarity between Jung's theory and *Field of Dreams*, she finally said, "I think you may have something there. Maybe you ought to do something with it." I knew I needed to sit down and write something, but, since I usually experienced a lot of resistance to writing, I decided first to present the ideas as a talk at a Jungian conference. The talk would force me to organize and elaborate my thoughts as well as allow me to test whether my ideas made sense or held any interest for other people. The story that follows is the result of those spontaneous thoughts.

I tell this story in the hope that some of the ideas contained here will have the same healing effect in the life of the reader as they have had in mine. I am mindful particularly of those who come to this book with a need to connect to a father whose loss or absence, actual or perceived, has in some way wounded their sense of wholeness. May they come away from this book with a stronger belief that healing is possible and a clearer picture of how they might proceed.

2   Blueprint For My Journey

Field of Dreams

When I started writing and teaching about *Field of Dreams*, my intention was to use the movie to explain Jung's psychology. By approaching the movie as a Jungian text, I was able to draw a deeper meaning out of an entertaining but perplexing movie. As I immersed myself in the deeper meaning of the movie's narrative, however, I began to feel a strange familiarity. The story of *Field of Dreams* was somehow my story. By writing and teaching about the movie, I developed a clear understanding of how I should continue my quest to find my father. *Field of Dreams* would provide the blueprint.

To help describe the amazing parallels between my journey and Ray Kinsella's journey, I must pause to explain how the movie captures concepts much larger than baseball and an Iowa cornfield. As a woman from Venezuela observed after visiting the Iowa field where the movie was filmed, "I did not understand the baseball. We do not have baseball in Bonaire, but I don't think the movie is so much about baseball as it is about other things."[1] Indeed, the movie is about other things, both profound and mythic. It captivates the imagination because it probes deep, archetypal themes that resonate within the psyche of the viewer. *Field of Dreams* is a dramatization of how the healing process of the human psyche functions.

To appreciate the deeper meaning of the film, it is helpful to approach the narrative as we would a dream; that is, as a composition containing both conscious and unconscious material.[2] Just as characters from "real life" assume symbolic significance in our dreams, so too in *Field of Dreams* the characters have a place in Ray Kinsella's conscious experience as well as a symbolic role to play in his inner life.

The film opens with a faded, sepia photograph of a young farm boy sitting in the middle of a field. A voice says, "My father's name was John Kinsella." Then through a series of old photographs, Ray Kinsella tells the story of his father and their life together. Ray's mother died when he was three. From then on, his father had to fill the roles of both mother and father. Although the movie offers few details of their life together, it is clear that there was some strong bonding mixed with areas of conflict. Both the bonding and the conflict revolved around baseball. John Kinsella, a former minor league player, shared his love of baseball with his son. As Ray tells us, "Instead of Mother Goose, I was put to bed with stories of Shoeless Joe." Shoeless Joe Jackson was John Kinsella's hero, a legendary player banned from baseball for his part in the 1919 Chicago White Sox scandal.

From the opening frames, it is clear that a fundamental theme of the movie is Ray's relationship with his father, but there is also a suggestion of some unresolved conflict resulting from that relationship. I did not understand the source of that conflict until later in the movie when Ray is riding home with Terrence Mann. Terrence asks Ray, "What happened to your father?" Ray answers, "He never made it as a baseball player so he tried to get his son to make it for him. By the time I was ten, playing baseball got to be like eating vegetables or taking out the garbage. So when I was fourteen, I started to refuse. Can you believe that—American boy refuses to have a catch with his father."

What I saw in this scene was the story of a father trying to share his dream with his son. At first, the son is content to play this role, but eventually it becomes a burden. With the coming of adolescence, the son expresses a need to differentiate himself from his father. This type of behavior reflects a typical process of ego development: a young man seeks an identity distinct from the one his father has imagined for him. As Ray grows older, the conflict intensifies. Ray tells Terrence Mann, "When I was seventeen, I packed my things, said something awful and left. After a while I wanted to come home but I didn't know how." Terrence asks, "What was the awful thing you said to your father?" Ray confesses, "I said I could never respect a man whose hero was a criminal." Ray knew that his father's hero, Shoeless Joe Jackson, was not a criminal. He said this just to get some distance from his father, but he also knew he hurt his father by saying what he did. Ray continues, "Son of a bitch died before I could take it back, before I could tell him. You know."

Field of Dreams is, therefore, about a son's need to reconnect to his dead father. Ray wants to tell his father he is sorry for the way he hurt him. Because I never knew my father, I identified with what I perceived to be Ray's deep need to make this connection with his father. The emptiness I felt because of my father's death was similar to the loss Ray felt because of the way he treated his father. Furthermore, the loss of our fathers—mine because of my father's early death and Ray's because of a foolish act of independence as an adolescent—had a lasting impact on our psyches.

When I viewed the movie through the lens of Jung's psychology, I realized that Ray Kinsella's character represents the conscious ego[3] and his father's character represents the father archetype, a fundamental structure within the collective unconscious.[4] This insight helped me understand how my father's death had such a profound impact on my psyche. Since the father archetype acquires con-

PSYCHE

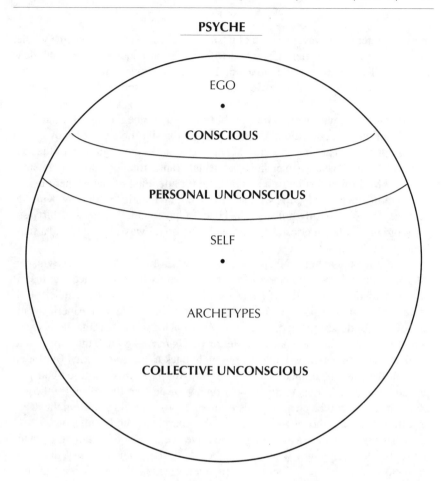

tent through contact with father figures, my father archetype was relatively empty with respect to my own father. My efforts to connect to my father were therefore attempts to give content to my inner father archetype so that I could become whole. By reflecting on *Field of Dreams*, I realized that my desire to connect to my father was actually an expression of my deeper self longing for wholeness.[5]

With the help of Jung's categories, I began to see Ray Kinsella's relationship with his father as a symbol for an inner dialogue between one's conscious ego and one's deeper self. In Ray Kinsella I saw a fellow orphan struggling to reconnect to his father in order to become whole. I interpreted Ray's longing to "come home" as a metaphor for becoming whole again, that is, reconnecting to the father archetype and healing the split between the ego and the deeper self. For Ray Kinsella, this journey home was a journey of reconciliation between the son and the father. For me, the journey home would involve connecting to my father in a completely new way. For each of us, it would be a journey to become whole, to become more completely integrated with the deepest source of personal identity. Once I recognized this fundamental similarity between my story and Ray Kinsella's, I returned to the movie to see what I might appropriate for my journey.

When the movie begins, Ray is thirty-six, at the beginning of what Jung would call mid-life transition.[6] Commenting on the significance of his own 36th year, Jung says, "The time is a critical one, for it marks the beginning of the second half of life, when a metanoia, a mental transformation, not infrequently occurs."[7] Mid-life transition is a natural time for attending to one's inner life and reintegrating neglected parts of the self. I could identify with Ray Kinsella because my own mid-life transition had been so profound. When I was thirty-six I was ordained a Jesuit priest. By the time I was forty, I was a husband and a stepfather with a completely new way of life.

The dramatic action of the movie begins when Ray hears a gentle whisper, "If you build it, he will come." At first, he can barely hear the voice, but then it becomes louder. When Ray first hears the voice, he is taking a quiet stroll through his cornfield at sunset. Later, I learned that in the Mexican American culture of the Southwest the cornfield or *milpa* is a place where spiritual things happen. It is not unusual for a native healer or *Curandera* to go into the cornfield to receive a healing message that is then brought back to the community. But for an Iowa farmer, this is strange business indeed. Ray is further confused and perplexed because he seems to be the only one who can hear the voice. By the end of the movie, it will be clear that this is an inner voice coming up from the deeper self, but initially the viewer shares in Ray's perplexity and confusion.

That night, while Ray is lying in bed, we see a flash of lightning over his house. For Jung, lightning is often a symbol for the beginning of a psychic transformation. "Lightning signifies a sudden, unexpected, and overpowering change of psychic condition."[8] It symbolizes a "transforming and healing function."[9] Right after the lightning we see Ray lying in bed next to his wife and once again we hear the voice: "If you build it, he will come." By applying Jung's interpretation to the movie, I gradually came to see the flash of lightning as a signal that the voice and its message marked the beginning of a process of inner transformation and healing. I was therefore more willing to trust the prompting of an inner voice in my own process of psychic healing.

Inner transformation, however, can also generate fear and anxiety, as the movie reveals in the very next scene. On the morning following the lightning flash and the reoccurrence of the voice, Ray walks into the kitchen where his daughter, Karin, is watching Jimmy Stewart in the movie, *Harvey*, the story of another man who heard voices. Ray's immediate reaction to seeing *Harvey* on the screen is to turn off the television. Karin protests that the movie is funny and asks her father why he turned off the television. Ray replies abruptly, "Trust me, Karin, it is not funny. The man is sick, very sick." Ray's strong reaction to seeing the movie *Harvey* reveals his initial attitude toward hearing inner voices: he is afraid he is going crazy. This concern is reinforced in the very next scene when Ray asks an old farmer whether he ever heard voices while working in the field. As Ray questions the old farmer about hearing voices, the song *Crazy* plays in the background while the other patrons in the farm supply store stare at Ray with suspicion.

These scenes from *Field of Dreams* helped me to appreciate how messages coming from one's inner self can initially trigger fears that they express some kind of sickness or craziness. Jung understood these fears as a common reaction to the onset of a process of inner transformation and healing. He wrote, "When a patient begins to feel the inescapable nature of his inner development, he may easily be overcome by a panic fear that he is slipping helplessly into some kind of madness he can no longer understand."[10] Ray Kinsella echoes this concern when he says at the beginning of the movie, "Until I heard the voice, I'd never done a crazy thing in my whole life."

What is crazy and what is sane is a question that recurs through the movie as it does in many experiences of inner transformation. Like Ray Kinsella, I was initially anxious about the inner messages rising from my unconscious and fearful about what they might mean for the stability of the rest of my life. I knew I was being called to do something to connect to my father, but I was anxious about what it might involve. Whenever these fears and anxieties began to stall my inner work, I found it very helpful to recall Jung's advice concerning messages from the inner self:

> This 'other being' is the other person in ourselves—that larger and greater personality maturing within us, the inner friend of the soul. You need not be insane to hear his voice. On the contrary, it is the simplest and most natural thing imaginable.[11]

Like Ray Kinsella, I would have to overcome my initial fears and gradually learn to listen to and trust the inner friend of my soul.

Ray is able to overcome his fear when the voice visits him a third time. Ray is once again working in his cornfield. He digs up a cornstalk and bends down to examine its roots. This time the voice speaks loudly and clearly, "If you build it, he will come." Angry and frustrated but finally willing to listen, Ray demands, "Who are you? What do you want from me?" Ray turns slowly in a full circle finally resting his eyes on a section of the cornfield adjoining his house. Gradually, as Ray stares at the field, the green grass of a baseball field replaces the corn. As Ray focuses on this image, it comes alive and a baseball player appears staring back at Ray. Ray interprets this vision as the answer to his question. He now understands the voice to mean, "If you build a baseball field, Shoeless Joe Jackson will get to come back and play ball again."

As I reflected on this scene, I was fascinated by the richness of its symbolism. Ray Kinsella is thirty-six years old. He is in the midst of a mid-life transition, a time when the psyche tries to reconnect to alienated aspects of the self. Ray hears a mysterious inner voice. By viewing Ray's character as a symbol for the conscious ego, I was able to understand the voice as arising spontaneously from the unconscious, expressing the inner longing of the self for wholeness and pointing the way. At first, the ego is troubled by this call from the self and resists the message, but eventually the ego listens and invites the self to say more, asking, "Who are you? What do you want from me?" Ray's story helped me to see the importance of learning to listen to the voice of the deeper self and learning to ask the kinds of questions that move one forward in the process of inner healing. As Clarissa Estes, a Jungian author, points out, "Asking the proper question is the central action of transformation—in fairytales, in analysis, and in individuation. Questions are the keys that cause the secret doors of the psyche to swing open."[12]

In Ray Kinsella's case, the psychic doors swing open to reveal a baseball field. The baseball field represents what Jung would call a mandala.[13] In situa-

MANDALA PATTERN OF BASEBALL FIELD

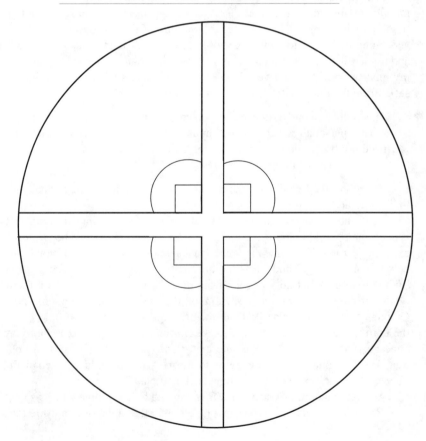

tions of inner conflict, the psyche will often produce a mandala not only to indicate that a resolution is possible, but also to provide a means of moving toward the goal. The appearance of the baseball field is a further message from the unconscious to the conscious ego: "If you consciously engage this symbol, if you build this mandala, the alienated dimension of the self, the father archetype, will reconnect with the ego."

The mandala offers a protective space within which the conflicted psychic elements are free to interact in a way that works their integration. The mandala provides a pattern of order that holds together the conflicted elements during the process of reconciliation and integration. By building the baseball field, Ray Kinsella will be able to reconnect to his father. The conflict between ego and father archetype will be resolved. The mandala symbolism of *Field of Dreams* taught me to be watchful for the appearance of mandala elements in my own journey to find my father.

Reflecting on the swift passage of time and the need to act before it is too late (typical mid-life concerns), Ray decides to obey the voice and build a baseball field in the middle of his cornfield. When he tries to explain why he is doing such a strange thing, he says it is "to right an old wrong." Ray means that in building the baseball field he will give Shoeless Joe Jackson a chance to play baseball again, thereby righting the wrong done to Shoeless Joe when he was banned from baseball. Ray's attempt to make sense of what he is about to do reveals a level of wisdom beyond his conscious awareness. Ray will indeed "right an old wrong," but it is deeper and more personal than the old wrong done to Shoeless Joe. The wrong Ray will right is the wrong he did to his father and more profoundly the wrong done to the inner self in the process of developing an independent and apparently separate ego. Ray has to heal that inner psychic wound to move forward with his life.

By building the baseball field, Ray will be engaged in a process of psychic healing that will not be immediately apparent on the level of conscious awareness. As is often the case in the conscious ego's relation to the unconscious, there is a deeper level of meaning in our actions that escapes the attention of ego-consciousness. Ray Kinsella's simple statement about righting an old wrong helped me to realize that there is at work in the psyche a level of wisdom beyond what we are able to consciously articulate and that we can trust this inner wisdom to guide us in the direction we must follow for our healing. Although I could not always explain clearly why I was doing some particular action that seemed related to my father, I knew that I was on the right track and that my efforts were worth whatever they cost.

So far in the movie, Ray has been primarily reactive in his response: he hears a voice, he asks a question, an image appears. This pattern symbolizes the initially reactive response of the conscious ego relative to the unconscious. But with the decision to build the baseball field, Ray becomes more actively engaged, initiating what Jung would call the exercise of active imagination.[14] The action of building the baseball field is a conscious, intentional engagement with an image originating in the unconscious. (The images in active imagination are usually provided by the unconscious in dreams or in reflective moments such as Ray strolling alone in his cornfield.) According to Jung, images are subjected to active imagination "for the purpose of restoring the broken connection between consciousness and the unconscious or integrating the latter's content."[15] For Ray Kinsella the activity of building the baseball field will restore the broken connection between the conscious ego and the father archetype and thereby heal the fragmentation within the unconscious.

By doing active imagination, Ray is learning to live a symbolic life; that is, he is allowing the images that come spontaneously from the unconscious to assume a symbolic role within conscious life. By engaging the image and doing something with it (like building the field), he is allowing the image to carry into conscious life the meaning it contains in the unconscious. The unconscious image is thus able to become a symbol and speak its meaning to consciousness. Active imagination creates a dialogue between consciousness and the unconscious that facilitates the flow of meaning between the two dimensions of psychic life.

Interpreting Ray's actions as an exercise in active imagination, I turned to *Field of Dreams* to learn how I might create a dialogue that would enable me to connect to my father. As I watched Ray begin to build his baseball field, I was struck by the obvious ritual overtones of his actions. As in many ritual acts, a story is told to accompany the action and give it meaning. In *Field of Dreams*, it is the story of a hero, Shoeless Joe, who was unjustly banned from baseball. The ritual texture of the story is enriched further because it is told as a father's response to his daughter's questions. As I listened to the question and answer dialogue of father and daughter, I could hear the echo of a Passover seder when the story of the liberation of Israel is told by the father in response to his children's questions. The use of ritual imagery transforms Ray's meticulous care in building his field into a quasi-sacred ritual guided by unseen forces.

The symbolic meaning of the work is heightened by contrasting it with the more practical considerations of consciousness. First, Ray plows under his cash crop to create space for the baseball field. As I watched Ray plow under the corn that was almost ripe for harvest and sale, I could see the craziness as well as the symbolic meaning in the act. By plowing under a valuable crop, Ray is in effect saying he is doing something that has a higher value. In the background, we can hear his more practical neighbors mocking this symbolic inner work and voicing the usual concerns of the ego, "Damn fool is going to lose his farm." Ray ignores these more practical considerations and moves forward with his symbolic work.

During the building Ray has little to support him except his inner vision and the assistance of his wife and daughter, but when the field is finished the value of the symbolic work begins to appear. In the middle of the completed field, Ray and his wife spread a blanket and share a celebratory evening meal. Stretched out on the blanket, Ray begins to tell his wife how his father used to tell him stories about Shoeless Joe. "Dad used to say no one could hit like Shoeless Joe," he says, recalling with obvious warmth and affection his childhood and the special times he spent with his father. Annie responds, "I think that is the first time I've ever seen you smile when you mention your father." Ray's smile and the obvious change in his attitude indicate that reconciliation between father and son is starting to take place and the split between ego and father archetype is beginning to heal. The symbolic work is beginning to pay off.

The evening meal in the middle of the field and the conversation about Ray's father and Shoeless Joe also add to the ritual overtones of the symbolic work. A ritual meal in which one tells stories received from earlier generations fits the pattern of what Jung would call a "totem meal, the purpose of which was to reunite the participants with the life of their ancestors."[16] Jung further points out that the Roman Catholic Mass is an example of a totem meal in which the story of the Last Supper of Jesus and his disciples is told to accompany the ritual act of eating bread and drinking a cup of wine.

When I realized the symbolic connections between Ray and Annie's shared meal in the baseball field and totem meals like the Mass, I became intrigued by the way Annie takes a chalice-shaped glass of wine and lifts it up with her two hands just like a priest at Mass. This simple act further adds to the ritual content of this special meal. The ritual of the totem meal effectively transforms the baseball field into symbolic sacred space.

At the end of the meal, Ray stands up and contemplates the field he has built. He remarks, "I've just created something totally illogical." More to the point, he has just created something completely symbolic, the logic of which transcends the narrow, rational pragmatism of ego-consciousness. By overcoming the practical considerations of the conscious ego and plowing under his cash crop, Ray has created a special symbolic place where he can do his inner work.

Watching Ray and Annie at their evening meal in the field and recalling how I would think of my father when I was celebrating Mass, I became more deeply aware of the power of symbol to move one beyond the limits of more practical everyday considerations. The ritual gesture of raising a cup of wine resonated in my unconscious and I could feel the flow of life-giving energy into consciousness. Within the ritual action of the Mass, I connected to my father's life. Through the symbolism and ritual of the Mass, he became alive in a way that transcended the limitations of human mortality. Ray Kinsella's sacred space helped me to recognize how I had connected to my father in the past and how I might deepen that connection in the future.

Ray's symbolic work of building the baseball field also helped me to appreciate what Jung was doing in building his famous Tower on his lakeside property at Bollingen. Jung said that this circular stone structure provided a place of spiritual concentration where he could live a symbolic life and actively relate to the symbols arising from the unconscious, free from the overly rationalistic requirements of ordinary life.[17] For Jung the tower was a physical representation in stone of the inner psychic work of becoming whole.

It is important to note why Jung chose to work in stone. At an earlier turning point in his life, Jung discovered that building little stone houses and castles "released a stream of fantasies" that facilitated his process of psychic healing.[18] Jung recalled that as a child, he had been fascinated by this kind of play. By returning to a similar kind of play as an adult, he found that it helped reestablish contact with the creative life of the small boy who continued to dwell inside. When Jung reflected on the significance of what he was doing, he noted that he was "doing it as if it were a rite." The important discovery for Jung was that a return to childhood memories could often be the beginning of contacting the deeper layers of the self.

When I looked at Ray's building of the baseball field and Jung's building of the Tower as parallel symbolic processes, I was able to identify and draw meaning from certain similar themes. Like Jung, Ray returns to the memories of his childhood and builds a baseball field as a first step in reconnecting to the deeper layers of the self. Furthermore, both the baseball field and the tower are mandala-shaped containers for the exercise of active imagination. Even the building of the field is carried out as though it were a sacred rite, further imitating Jung's approach to inner work. Ray Kinsella and Jung heightened my awareness of the value of learning to live a symbolic life. They also provided concrete examples of how one might do symbolic work through active imagination, mandala symbolism and a return to early childhood play.

The picture of active imagination presented in *Field of Dreams* is also faithful to the Jungian model in highlighting the essential period of waiting that follows the building of the field. After the activity of building the field, there follows a period of intense concentration on the image and attentive waiting for the unconscious to act. Jung describes the purpose of this period in the following words:

> [A]ctive imagination, as the term denotes, means that the images have a life of their own and that the symbolic events develop according to their own logic—that is, of course, if your conscious reason does not interfere. You begin by concentrating upon a starting point...[W]hen you concentrate on a mental picture, it begins to stir, the image becomes enriched by details, it moves and develops...And so when we concentrate on an inner picture and when we are careful not to interrupt the natural flow of events, our unconscious will produce a series of images which make a complete story.[19]

True to the Jungian model, Ray concentrates on the baseball field, watching it contemplatively through the passing seasons and waiting patiently for the story to unfold. Rising from his bed in the middle of the night, Ray looks out at the baseball field and says confidently, "Something's gonna happen out there; I can feel it." In the next scene it is winter. As his family gathers in the background to celebrate Christmas, Ray sits all alone at the window wistfully watching the baseball field fill up with snow.

These scenes helped me to realize the importance of contemplation in the exercise of active imagination. It is not enough to do something symbolic. One must then wait attentively and allow the unconscious to work. Active imagination is an inner dialogue that must respect the relative contributions of both the conscious and unconscious dimensions of the psyche. Whenever I would become impatient with the rhythm of the process of inner healing, I would find it helpful to recall the image of Ray Kinsella sitting at his window and the words of Jung. If one concentrates on a mental image and keeps conscious reason from interfering with the natural flow of events, eventually the unconscious will be able to reveal its healing story.

What happens next in Ray Kinsella's story is so dense in symbolic content that the most effective way to explain its impact on me is to describe the sequence of events and then summarize the meaning I was able to draw from it.

Ray Kinsella contemplates his baseball field and gradually the unconscious begins to reveal pieces of a story. A year of attentive waiting has passed and it is summer once again. The sounds of a televised baseball game can be heard in the background. The tension between the demands of the outer practical world and the value of the inner symbolic world is about to reach a crisis point when something extraordinary happens.

Ray and Annie are sitting at the dining room table discussing their financial situation. Annie reminds Ray that the baseball field has reduced the amount of land they have for producing income. Ray responds, "So what are you saying; we can't keep the field?" "Makes it real hard to keep the farm," Annie answers, highlighting the tension between the practical concerns of the conscious ego and the work of the deeper self.

While Ray and Annie are talking, their daughter keeps interrupting, trying to get Ray's attention. Finally, Ray asks, "What is it?" Karin answers softly, "There's a man out there on your lawn." Ray looks out the window and there stands Shoeless Joe Jackson in the middle of the baseball field. Ray goes out on the porch and flips on the overhead lights illuminating the field and Shoeless Joe. Ray walks on to the field and Joe signals Ray to hit to him. Without saying a word, Ray picks up a bat and tries to hit a ball to Shoeless Joe, but his first attempt to connect fails. Ray looks at Joe and says meekly, "Sorry." Ray tries again, this time reaching Shoeless Joe. After catching several balls, Joe asks Ray whether he knows how to pitch. Ray goes to the pitcher's mound and Joe goes to the batter's box. As Ray begins to wind-up he says to himself with irrepressible joy and amazement, "I am pitching to Shoeless Joe Jackson."

When they finish playing, Ray and Joe walk toward each other and begin to speak. Joe tells Ray that being banned from baseball was like having a part of himself amputated. He would have played for nothing, he confesses. It was the game that he loved. Then, as Annie and Karin come toward the field, Ray and Joe walk toward them. Joe looks down at the gravel boundary of the field and stops. Karin asks innocently, "Are you a ghost?" Joe answers, "What do you think?" "You look real to me," Karin says. "Well then, I guess I'm real," Joe responds.

Annie invites Joe to come into the house. Joe looks down at the gravel boundary and says, "I don't think I can." Then, Joe asks if he can come back and bring some of the other Chicago White Sox with him. "I built this for you," Ray says, "They're all welcome here." As Joe walks back toward the outfield, he turns and asks, "Is this heaven?" "No," Ray says with a smile, "it's Iowa." Then, Joe disappears into the tall corn that grows along the edge of the outfield. Ray turns to Annie. "We're keeping this field," he says. "You bet your ass we are," she says, hugging him.

When I interpreted the foregoing scenes as I would a dream, the symbolic meaning of the various images began to unfold. First, I was struck by the archetypal imagery in the scenes. By building the baseball field and then concentrating on this mandala-shaped symbol, Ray has allowed the unconscious to produce the image of Shoeless Joe. Shoeless Joe is an archetypal hero figure who emerges from the collective unconscious[20] (represented by the cornfield) and enters into dialogue with the ego within the protective psychic space provided by the mandala. The little girl, Karin, is the first one to see Shoeless Joe. In effect, she introduces Shoeless Joe to her father, thereby fulfilling one of the key roles of the anima archetype, i.e., introducing the conscious ego to archetypal figures coming from the deeper levels of the collective unconscious.[21]

When I first started unpacking the symbolism of these scenes, I had difficulty deciding which feminine character, the daughter or the wife, functions most like an anima figure. Then, I realized that the anima facilitates communication between the ego and the collective unconscious by creating a bridge between conscious life and the deeper layers of the unconscious. If the anima functions like a bridge between the collective unconscious and the ego, then we can see both Karin and Annie forming together a composite anima archetype. The daughter Karin represents the segment of the bridge that is rooted in the mythic possibilities of the collective unconscious and the wife Annie represents the part of the bridge that connects to the concerns of the ego. Both Karin and Annie fulfill the symbolic functions of an anima figure by supporting Ray's efforts to respond to the call of the unconscious; Annie however, expresses more of the practical concerns of the ego while Karin manifests a more intimate rapport with the archetypal figures arising from the collective unconscious. It is Annie who points out that building the field has placed their ownership of the farm at risk, thus questioning to some extent the wisdom of doing symbolic work. Karin, on the other hand, is her father's constant companion in the construction of the field, sharing in his stories about the accomplishments and relative innocence of Shoeless Joe.

Karin is not only the first to see Shoeless Joe, but also the one who confirms the reality of this archetypal figure. "You look real to me," she says. Karin's statement is fundamental to a Jungian interpretation of the reality of unconscious material. According to Jung, "It is essential that we do not detract from the reality of the unconscious, and that the figures of the unconscious be understood as real and effective factors."[22] Shoeless Joe is real in the sense that the archetypal image of the hero is truly effective in the structure of Ray's psychic life. It is the role of the anima to affirm the reality of this psychic entity and to assist the ego in connecting to it. Together Karin and Annie reflect both the positive value and the practical costs of doing symbolic work.

When I reflected on the role of the anima and its possible significance in my own journey to connect to my father, I was reminded of the journey I took with Michelle to visit my father's grave and the impact it had on me. If the role of the anima is to function as a bridge to the archetypal levels of the unconscious, then Michelle's presence at my father's grave could be interpreted as the presence of an anima figure serving as a bridge to the deeper levels of the psychic pain resulting from my father's death. Because of Michelle's presence, I was able to connect to that pain in a way that I had never before experienced. The presence of the anima helped me to feel the pain of the emptiness in my father archetype that resulted from my father's absence. What I expressed through my convulsive tears was the deep sorrow that I felt at the loss of my father, but I was also feeling the flow of healing energy from the deeper layers of the unconscious. The presence of an anima figure was supporting and facilitating the communication between my conscious ego and the deeper self that was guiding the healing process. Since Michelle had been so instrumental in helping me connect to the deeper levels of my loss, I knew she would continue to play an important role in my journey to find my father.

Having clarified the archetypal meaning and symbolism of Ray's wife and daughter, I then turned to the characters of Shoeless Joe and the other baseball players who eventually appear on the field. Shoeless Joe and the other Chicago White Sox players are examples of the archetype of the hero, more specifically, the hero who falls from grace and stands in need of redemption. These mythic figures come up from the collective unconscious and enter the mandala, where they become accessible to consciousness.

According to Jung, universal archetypal patterns acquire specific content in an individual's psychic life based on the personal history and conscious experience of the individual. It is, therefore, not surprising that the archetypal theme of fall and redemption finds concrete expression in Ray's inner life with the story of the Chicago White Sox who were accused of throwing the 1919 World Series. By allowing the theme of fall and redemption to emerge from the unconscious and by actively engaging the story in imagination (interacting with Joe and the other players), Ray is participating in his own redemptive process and return to grace.

"I am pitching to Shoeless Joe Jackson" means that, through the exercise of active imagination, Ray is truly engaged with the story of Shoeless Joe and the Chicago White Sox. Through this engagement, the archetypal energy associated with this story becomes available to conscious life. When one consciously engages the archetypal story through active imagination, a healing process begins to take place in the psyche. Split-off aspects of the self are brought back into relationship, thereby releasing their energies into psychic life.

Shoeless Joe's reference to an amputated part of himself points to Ray's severance of part of the self and consequent loss of wholeness. In developing a conscious ego, Ray split off a significant aspect of his unconscious life, the father archetype. According to Jung, "The 'merely conscious' man who is all ego is a mere fragment, in so far as he seems to exist apart from the unconscious."[23] The ego separated from the father archetype is in a state of psychic fragmentation that must eventually be healed. Ray is only a fragment of his potentially whole self because he has cut himself off from the energy associated with the father archetype.

The restoration of Shoeless Joe and the other White Sox to the game of baseball is a symbolic enactment of Ray's own process of redemption. For Ray, bringing back Shoeless Joe is more than just an act of penance, as Terrence Mann later suggests; it is an integral step in the inner process of reconciliation. According to Jung, a legend or myth "grips the hearer because the story gives expression to parallel processes in his own unconscious which in that way are integrated with consciousness again."[24] Ray is gripped by the legend of Shoeless Joe and the 1919 Chicago White Sox because it expresses his own inner fall from grace and need for redemption. There is a parallel process between Ray's personal story and the legend of Shoeless Joe. Shoeless Joe's sin was that he took money for something that was meant to be a game. For Joe, playing the game was like a sacred rite, but he profaned it by taking money from the gamblers. Joe's atonement lies, therefore, in playing the game once again for pure fun. Ray's sin was breaking the relationship with his father and with that part of the self that is identified with the father, the father archetype. Ray's redemption will therefore lie in reestablishing communication with the father archetype.

It is significant that Ray's first word to Shoeless Joe is "Sorry," the very word that Ray wishes he had been able to say to his father before he died. By engaging with Shoeless Joe and saying he is sorry, Ray begins a process of reconciliation with the father archetype. Since Ray finalized his separation from his father by maligning Shoeless Joe, it is only fitting that the first step in Ray's own redemption is to reconnect to his father's hero and restore the fallen hero to grace.

When I reflected on the possible significance of the hero archetype for my own journey, I realized that the image of my father as a Marine and a war hero had exercised a powerful hold on my imagination since childhood. I recalled how as a small child I used to stand in front of a mirror wearing my father's Marine cap and how as a young adult I had almost enlisted in the Marine Corps because of the symbolism surrounding the image of the Marine/Warrior. Like Ray Kinsella, I had given specific content to my hero archetype based on my own personal history. Also like Ray Kinsella, my hero archetype was closely associated with my father. Ray Kinsella had connected to his hero archetype by building a baseball field. If I wanted to follow the blueprint laid out in *Field of Dreams*, I would have to find some way to connect to the Marines in order to access whatever healing energy might still be available to me through this hero archetype. Since becoming a Marine/Warrior was no longer a viable option, I would have to find ways to open and expand the hero archetype to include elements with which I might more readily identify.

I also realized that the reason I was so deeply affected by the story of Ray Kinsella, his father and Shoeless Joe was because it resonated with a parallel process within my own psychic life. Just as the story of Shoeless Joe gave expression to Ray Kinsella's unconscious process, so too Ray Kinsella's story expressed key elements of my own psychic journey. Jung's comment on parallel processes helped me to understand why simply watching *Field of Dreams* released such a strong flow of psychic energy into my consciousness. My intense emotional reaction to the movie was the result of the deep archetypal energies that were tapped by the movie's images.

In addition to demonstrating how archetypal images facilitate the flow of healing energy from the unconscious into consciousness, the foregoing scenes from the movie also contained two images that would help me to facilitate more effectively the dialogue between consciousness and the unconscious. These images were: 1) Ray switching on the overhead lights to illuminate the baseball field and reveal Shoeless Joe and 2) Joe stopping at the field's gravel boundary.

Switching the lights on the field is a visual representation of what Jung would call illumination (Latin, *illuminatio*), casting the light of consciousness on material coming from the unconscious. In dreams, illumination is often represented by images of light such as the sun or moon, but as Jung points out, "Illumination ('a light dawns,' 'it is becoming clear,' etc.) can be expressed just as well or even better in modern dreams by switching on the electric light."[25]

Jung uses the term "illumination" to refer to the kind of clarification or enlightenment that comes from submitting unconscious data to the light of consciousness. By using this term, Jung intends to distinguish illumination from the kind of clarification that comes merely from the exercise of consciousness without any reference or attention to unconscious data. The type of clarification that eschews any reference to the unconscious Jung defined as intellectual or rational elucidation. Jung contrasts illumination with elucidation to illustrate that working with the unconscious calls for a different type of knowing and seeing than that which is employed when working in the realm of consciousness.

In *Field of Dreams*, the process of active imagination illuminates the protective psychic space of the mandala and reveals the archetype of the hero. By inviting the unconscious into dialogue, consciousness is eventually able to "cast light on" (illuminate) the unconscious material. Illuminating the field to reveal Shoeless Joe is the first of two significant instances in which throwing light on the field symbolizes what Jung means by the illumination of unconscious material. The second instance will come at the end of the movie when Annie, the anima figure, switches on the lights to illuminate Ray and his father having a catch in the middle of the field, thus symbolizing the ultimate reconciliation of the ego with the father archetype.

When I applied the image of illumination to my own inner journey, I realized the image opened a pathway to a different kind of knowing and seeing. Strictly on the level of conscious experience, my father and I had never met, but within the inner psychic space created through active imagination, there resided the possibility of a kind of knowing and seeing that could go beyond the narrow confines of conscious experience. By inviting the unconscious into dialogue with consciousness, I might be able to see the symbolic meaning of certain persons and events in a way that transcended mere rational elucidation, thus opening up the possibility of an experience of illumination or enlightenment wherein I might truly meet my father. As I proceeded on my journey, I would try to stay alert to the possibility of finding such illumination in the persons and events I encountered.

While the appearance of Shoeless Joe on the baseball field symbolized for me the transcendent possibilities of active imagination, the image of Shoeless Joe stopping at the gravel boundary of the field provided me with a valuable lesson in the necessary limitations of any dialogue between consciousness and the unconscious. Active imagination is a method that facilitates the interplay of conscious and unconscious material, but if the method is to be successful in its work of integration, the distinction between consciousness and the unconscious must be maintained. The boundary of the field is significant in that it contains the protected area within which the unconscious and active imagination are allowed free play. Beyond this protective boundary, the regulative structures of conscious experience hold sway.

According to Jung, a mandalic enclosure like the baseball field functions as a *temenos*, an isolated sacred place: "The circle in this case protects or isolates an inner content or process that should not get mixed up with things outside."[26] The purpose of these "protective walls" is "to prevent an outburst or disintegration."[27] If Joe had left the field and entered the house with Ray, it would have represented the beginnings of a psychotic episode, a loss of the distinction between conscious and unconscious material. In order for integration to take place, the distinction between conscious and unconscious must be maintained. A creative and healing integration of unconscious material is made possible by recognizing both the power and the limitations of active imagination. Instead of psychosis, the result is a healthy relationship between ego and self.

Effective active imagination requires a permeable but stable conscious personality. The conscious personality must be permeable enough to allow engagement with images coming from the unconscious, but stable enough to hold the unconscious images within the protective psychic space of active imagination and not be overwhelmed by the unconscious. In *Field of Dreams*, the permeability of the conscious personality is dramatized when Ray crosses the gravel boundary and walks onto the baseball field. The stability of the conscious personality is symbolized when Shoeless Joe stops at the gravel boundary, indicating that he is not allowed to leave the field.

As a child, I used to daydream about my father coming home someday. I would run up to him and throw my arms around him. He would explain that the news of his death had been a mistake and he was happy to be home again with my mother and me. The image of Shoeless Joe stopping at the gravel boundary helped me to realize the difference between that childhood fantasy and what I was now trying to do through active imagination. Just as Shoeless Joe could never go into the house with Ray and Annie to have a cup of coffee, my father would never come through the door and put his arms around me. Clinging to such a desire would impede my healing because it denied the limits of conscious experience. Nevertheless, active imagination could offer an opportunity to connect to my father in a way that was just as real in terms of its effectiveness for my psychological healing and wholeness. Although my father would never come home from the war the way I once wished as a child, I could still meet him if I remained faithful to my inner work and accepted the necessary limitations of that work.

With a clearer understanding of the role of archetypes and the dynamic interaction of consciousness and the unconscious within active imagination, I returned to the movie's narrative to see what else I could learn. Shoeless Joe and the other Chicago White Sox eventually become regular visitors to Ray's field. We see a scene of the White Sox having fun playing baseball, while Ray and Karin sit in the bleachers enjoying the banter of the players. For me, this scene captured an image of the ego and an anima figure joined together in a re-creative dialogue with the archetypal hero figures that have emerged from the collective unconscious. The scene thereby indicates that a significant stage of development has been reached in the individuation process and that the ego is beginning to enjoy this level of integration; as Ray says, "I was having a fun day, a good day." But just as the ego starts to get comfortable with this stage in the process, the inner voice returns to disturb the equilibrium and to initiate a new phase of development. Ray hears the voice say, "Ease his pain." Ray's immediate reaction is once again annoyance and confusion. He asks, frustrated, "Whose pain? What pain?" Greeted with silence, he says disgustedly to the voice, "Thanks a lot."

What I discerned in the reappearance of the voice was a reminder to stay open to the rhythm of equilibrium and disequilibrium that characterizes the process of individuation. As Jungian analyst Edward Edinger points out, "Individuation is a process, not a realized goal. Each new level of integration must submit to further transformation if development is to proceed."[28] The return of the voice introduces the disequilibrium that will move the process forward.

Ray's reaction to the voice expresses the natural tendency of the ego to prefer to rest in the enjoyment of what has already been achieved rather than continue the process of transformation.

As I recalled earlier experiences of healing, I realized that often I thought the work was complete, that I had healed what needed to be healed, but then something would come along to show me there was more work to be done. I could easily sympathize with Ray's resistance to a further stage of work, but I also recognized that the rhythm of equilibrium/disequilibrium is the usual pattern of psychological growth and development and that I would have to be patient with this pattern as I moved forward on my journey.

Eventually, Ray accepts the rhythm of the process. Ray understands the voice to mean that he must go to Boston to find Terrence Mann and take him to a baseball game. Annie's immediate response to this new mission expresses the concerns of practical reason. "You cannot take off for Boston while you're going broke in Iowa," she tells Ray. Ray's answer reveals he is beginning to appreciate the mystery and depth of the individuation process. He replies, "Annie, this is really new territory for both of us, I know, but we're dealing with primal forces of nature here. When primal forces of nature tell you to do something, the prudent thing is not to quibble over details."

By engaging the unconscious in dialogue, ego-consciousness has become more open to the deeper archetypal levels of the collective unconscious, those primordial structures that give access to the primal forces of psychic life. Ray and Annie realize that they are operating on a deeper archetypal level when they discover that they had the same dream the night before. For Jung, this kind of meaningful coincidence is an example of synchronicity.[29] When one descends to the level of the collective unconscious through inner dialogue with archetypal figures, one becomes open to a level of perception or cognition that transcends the usual space-time limitations of conscious experience.

In *Field of Dreams*, the synchronicity of the shared dream was precisely the evidence Annie needed to be convinced of the value of Ray's trip to Boston. "I'll help you pack," she says. For me the synchronicity of the dream signaled the possibility of a kind of perception or cognition that is not limited by space or time. Since the separation between my father and me was primarily a separation in space and time, the synchronicity of the dream pointed to a kind of knowing that might be able to overcome the separation between my father and me. Ray and Annie's synchronous dream gave me cause to hope that through a meaningful coincidence of events I might be guided on my journey and someday meet my father in a way that was not limited by our separation in space and time.

The movie's narrative continues with Ray's decision to go to Boston to find Terrence and take him to a baseball game. Ray's attitude toward this journey is that of a pilgrim. "I won't even stay in motels; I'll sleep in the car, I'll beg for food," he says, thus imitating the trust of a medieval pilgrim. By assuming the attitude of a pilgrim, Ray transforms the trip to Boston into a symbolic journey or pilgrimage that expands the protective, psychic space of the mandala and active imagination. The physical journey continues the symbolic work that began with the building of the baseball field.

In an excellent book on the parallels between Carl Jung and Theresa of Avila, John Welch explains the close relationship between a physical pilgrimage and an inner journey of transformation.[30] A pilgrim leaves behind the routines and responsibilities of everyday life in order to search out sacred places and symbols to aid the inner transformation and search for wholeness. In *Field of Dreams*, Ray leaves behind his wife and daughter and the financial difficulties of the farm and travels halfway across the country to go to a baseball game at Boston's Fenway Park, a shrine in baseball mythology.

Ray's trip also conforms to the pattern of a symbolic journey or pilgrimage in that a pilgrim trusts in the ultimate value of the journey even though its final goal remains unclear until the journey is completed. Ray is convinced that he has to make this journey, but he doesn't know why. "I feel it," Ray says, "I feel it as strongly as I've ever felt anything in my life. There's a reason. I think something's going to happen at the game. I don't know what, but there's something at Fenway Park in Boston, and I have to be there with Terrence Mann to find it." Although Ray does not realize it at the time, this is the first leg on a symbolic journey that will finally bring him "home" to a deeper sense of wholeness. The ultimate goal of a pilgrimage is not to arrive at some physical destination but to "come home" to the self, the center of our psychic lives.

Through Ray Kinsella's pilgrimage, I was able to recognize a further symbolic significance in my trip with Michelle to visit my father's grave. Besides being a journey in the presence of my anima figure, it was also a pilgrimage to a sacred place. I felt compelled to make this trip even though I did not understand its purpose until we arrived. All I knew was that I needed to go to the Catskill Mountains and that I needed to go with Michelle. Although it was a physical journey, its ultimate goal was not a physical destination but an inner transformation. The external travelling became the occasion for my inner healing. Once I became aware of the healing potential of a pilgrimage, I began to look for other physical journeys that might lead me "home" to my father.

On his pilgrimage, Ray Kinsella meets two characters who provide wisdom and guidance for his journey to wholeness, Terrence Mann and Doc Graham. These two characters represent examples of what Jung would call the archetype of the wise old man.[31] The wise old man usually appears as an authority figure, like a doctor, priest, teacher, or professor and is closely associated with the father archetype in the psychological development of a son.

As I searched for possible wise old man archetypes in my own life, I recalled how I was drawn to certain priests and professors as models in my efforts to discern a direction for my life. I could remember sitting in college classes listening to Jesuit philosophy professors, being impressed by their wisdom and integrity, and wanting to be like them. I was also aware at the time that part of their attraction for me was that I saw in them worthy substitutes for my father.

According to Jung, the wise old man can be a stand-in for the father in the dreams of a son, assuming the role of an " 'informing spirit' who initiates the dreamer into the meaning of life and explains its secrets according to the teachings of old."[32] The wise old man is therefore a source of wisdom for an individual, particularly during those times when one is searching for meaning and direction. Ray Kinsella found a potential wise old man in Terrence Mann, the writer and civil rights leader, but Terrence's first response to Ray is to refuse the role of wise old man. He tells Ray, "I can't tell you the secret of life, and I don't have any answers for you. I just want to be left alone."

In order to move forward on his journey, Ray must first overcome the reluctance of his guide. When Ray asks Terrence why he stopped writing and being involved, he learns that it was due to the deaths of Robert Kennedy and Martin Luther King. Terrence explains:

> I was the East Coast distributor of 'involved.' I ate it, drank it, and breathed it. Then they killed Martin. They killed Bobby. And they elected Tricky Dick. Twice. And now, people like you think I must be miserable that I'm not involved anymore. Well, I've got news for you: I spent all my misery years ago. I have no more pain for any of you. I gave at the office.

What I heard in Terrence Mann's lament was an expression of the meaning and purpose that political and civil rights leaders like Kennedy and King had given to his life. Their untimely deaths cut him off from this source of meaning and strength. Jung would describe this experience as a loss of connection to the king archetype.[33] The king archetype symbolizes that inner source of commitment and passion that gives meaning and purpose to a man's creativity. By identifying with leaders like Kennedy and King, Terrence Mann had connected to an inner source of commitment and passion that gave meaning to his writing and involvement in the civil rights movement. When they were killed, he lost all enthusiasm for his work.

Although Terrence at first refused to give any advice on the secret of life, he taught Ray through the story of Kennedy and King about an inner source of psychic energy that informs one's creativity. The reluctant wise old man thereby began to fill the role of advisor and teacher.

It was easy for me to identify with Terrence Mann's experience. In the summer of 1963, I read Theodore H. Whyte's *Making of the President*. I was nineteen years old and desperately seeking a model to give direction to my life. The image of John F. Kennedy filled that role. I saw in Kennedy the kind of man my father might have become: an Irish Catholic war hero who returned home to live a life of public service. I returned to college in the fall determined to get a job in Kennedy's next campaign. When Kennedy was shot, it felt like my own father was being killed again. I still recall the anger and disappointment I felt that day as I struggled to understand what had happened. The news of Kennedy's death felt like a blow that completely wiped out any enthusiasm I might have had for a career in politics.

What I learned from Terrence Mann's story was the importance of archetypal figures in helping one to stay connected to an inner source of commitment and passion. I also recognized the close connection between the archetypes of father, king and wise old man. In Jungian terms, wholeness requires the ego to be connected to the psychic energies associated with the archetypes of father and king and the archetype of wise old man acts as an intermediary in the process of integration. Together the archetypes give meaning and strength to a man's identity and help him to access his own creativity. Men who, through death, separation, abuse, or affective inaccessibility, have lost connection with their inner king and father figures are often faced with the task in mid-life of overcoming the negative effects of that loss on their creativity. *Field of Dreams* taught me the value of using active imagination and other kinds of inner work to reestablish the connection.

My own efforts to reconnect to the archetypes of king and father were helped by spending several evenings walking slowly around Dealey Plaza in Dallas, Texas, trying to relive in my imagination the events surrounding Kennedy's death. I stood on the grassy knoll and imagined Kennedy's car passing by. Then I walked into the roadway and stood for a moment on the very spot where Kennedy was shot. I was trying to be as present as possible to the moment of his death. When I returned home, I placed an autographed campaign photograph of Kennedy next to a photograph of my father on a bookshelf overlooking the desk where I write. Through practices like these, I have been able to heal some of the trauma resulting from the double loss of king and father and thereby revive the creative energy and enthusiasm I know I lost on November 22, 1963.

I also found in Terrence Mann a symbol for the role that writing and storytelling play in psychological transformation and healing. Ray describes Terrence as a "warm and gentle voice of reason during a time of great madness," who now writes interactive children's videos that "teach kids to resolve their conflicts peacefully." I interpreted this description to mean that, in times of psychological stress and turmoil, writing and storytelling can bring peace and order to unconscious conflicts by allowing them to emerge into the light of conscious reason.

The healing work of writing and storytelling is particularly powerful when it draws on myths that arise from the collective unconscious. *Field of Dreams* dramatizes this relation of writing and storytelling to the collective unconscious when Shoeless Joe Jackson, the archetypal hero figure, invites Terrence Mann, the writer, to visit the mythic baseball heroes in the mysterious region from whence they come. The originating realm of the archetypal hero figures is the collective unconscious represented by the tall corn growing beyond the baseball field. Terrence Mann receives this unique privilege because he will write about what he finds in the cornfield. Looking toward the tall corn, Terrence says,

"There is something out there. If I have the courage to do it, what a story it will make." When Ray asks Terrence if he will write about his experience, Terrence answers, "You bet I'll write about it. That's what I do." Writing and storytelling are thus presented as the admission ticket into the healing mysteries of the collective unconscious.

The character of Terrence Mann, therefore, represents a capacity within the self to tap into the rich reservoir of the collective unconscious to heal psychological wounds and resolve inner conflicts through writing and storytelling. The image of Terrence Mann, laughing as he stepped cautiously into the cornfield, encouraged me to explore the possibility of using writing and storytelling as a way to connect to my father.

The second wise old man that Ray meets on his pilgrimage is Doc Graham. For me, Doc Graham embodied several additional aspects of the healing power of the self. When Ray asks Doc Graham whether he regrets having played only five minutes in major league baseball, Doc Graham answers, "If I had only gotten to be a doctor for five minutes, that would have been a tragedy." Doc Graham thus teaches Ray that the real tragedy in life is not some missed opportunity, but rather the failure to realize that a permanent capacity for healing resides in the psyche. In Doc Graham's words, I found the consolation of realizing that in the psychological realm there is always the possibility for healing.

Doc Graham also shows that the healing effects of the self reach beyond the psyche into everyday life. The practical impact of the healing power of the self is dramatized when Doc Graham steps across the gravel boundary of the baseball field to revive Ray's daughter, Karin, who has fallen from the bleachers. Since Karin is also an anima figure, I saw too in Doc Graham a symbol for what Jung referred to as *cura animarum*, the care and healing of the soul.

Doc Graham thus became for me a reassuring symbol that we have within us the capacity to doctor our souls and care for our inner lives so that the healing effects flow into our everyday lives. Although I never had an opportunity to meet my father in this life, I was confident that the healing effects of my inner work could overcome the negative impact of that loss.

The character of Doc Graham also represents the timeless nature of the self because of the way he freely moves backward and forward in time. The first time Ray meets Doc Graham he has to travel backward in time to 1972. Soon afterward, Ray picks up the young Archie Graham who is setting out to begin his brief career as a minor league baseball player. Doc Graham's final appearance comes in the present time of the movie when he leaves the baseball field to save Karin. The young Archie Graham actually transforms into old Doc Graham as he crosses the gravel boundary of the baseball field. Such movement back and forth through time visually illustrates the relative timelessness of the archetypal layers of the unconscious. According to Robert Johnson, "There is a common quality that runs through the symbols of the Wise Man—a feeling of wisdom that transcends generations, agelessness in the sense of being outside the flow of time."[34]

By showing the character of Archie/Doc Graham travelling back and forth across the boundaries of time, the movie presents a cinematic image of Jung's theory that "the psychic life of the archetype is timeless in comparison with our individual time-boundedness."[35]

Ray and Annie's synchronous dream taught me to hope that there might be a way for me to know my father that transcends the limitations of space and time. Doc Graham's travelling back and forth through time reinforced that hope by revealing the timeless quality of the archetypal level of the self. Together these two images pointed toward the timeless nature of the inner self and thus opened an additional pathway for me to explore in my journey to connect to my father.

As I followed the narrative of Ray Kinsella's pilgrimage, another image gradually emerged for me. In the background of Ray's interactions with Terrence Mann and Doc Graham, a subtle sequence of images came together to reveal a pattern of descent and ascent.

The pattern begins when Ray and Terrence are talking about the impact of the deaths of Kennedy and King on Terrence's life and work. This is the conversation in which Terrence begins to assume the role of wise old man on Ray's pilgrimage. The conversation takes place as the two descend a winding ramp leading to the bleachers at Fenway Park. Sitting in the bleachers watching the game together, Ray and Terrence then receive a message that sends them to Chisolm, Minnesota to find Moonlight Graham. When Ray and Terrence arrive in Chisolm, they go immediately to a phone booth to look for the name of Moonlight Graham in the directory. Behind the phone booth is a set of stairs ascending from one street level to the next. Later, Ray and Moonlight/Doc Graham are shown walking together at the top of this same stairway.

Although the pattern was subtle, it conveyed for me a clear image of descent and ascent. The sequence of images caught my attention because they are so similar to the symbolic movement that accompanies the narrative of Dante's *Divine Comedy*. Dante descends into the underworld in the company of his guide, Virgil, and then climbs the mountain of purgatory to enter the wisdom of paradise in the company of another guide, St. Bernard. Ray Kinsella's descent with Terrence Mann and ascent with Moonlight/Doc Graham is a modern parallel to Dante's symbolic journey.

From a Jungian perspective, this archetypal pattern of descent and ascent is another way to describe the dialogue between the ego and the self. The ego descends into the underworld of the unconscious to encounter the images that tell the psyche's inner story. The ego ascends upward when it allows the images from the unconscious to become symbolic and thus carry their meaning into conscious life. Together the two images represent the conscious ego descending into the inner world of the unconscious in order to rise up to a higher level of conscious awareness and insight. The pattern of descent and ascent thus becomes a way to express the psyche's inner movement toward wholeness.

The pattern of descent and ascent present in Ray Kinsella's journey with

Terrence Mann and Doc Graham showed me how his pilgrimage continued the dialogue between the ego and the self that began with the symbolic work of building the baseball field. The image presented in *Field of Dreams* taught me to be watchful for similar patterns of descent and ascent in my own symbolic journey to connect to my father. The presence of Terrence Mann and Doc Graham also inspired me to trust that comparable wisdom figures might appear to accompany and guide me on my journey.

Ray Kinsella's symbolic journey reaches its conclusion when he returns home in the company of his two guides. "We're coming home," he tells Annie on the phone, thereby stating clearly the ultimate purpose of pilgrimage—the ego's coming home to the center of psychic life, the self. When Ray arrives home, he finds that the baseball field has acquired a life of its own. The field is now filled with the heroes of old playing a whole baseball game. The symbolic work of active imagination and pilgrimage has allowed the unconscious to produce a whole story within the mandala's protective psychic space. When Terrence sees the baseball field and all the old-time baseball players, his one-word response is, "Unbelievable!" Ray adds, "It's more than that, it's perfect."

What I heard in Ray's words was an expression of the vitality, energy and wholeness that the ego experiences as the fruit of symbolic work. The ego is therefore beginning to realize the value of living a symbolic life, but just as the psyche is about to enter a new level of integration, an internal debate arises to challenge the value of symbolic work.

On one side of the debate stands Annie's brother, Mark. From his first appearance, Mark has challenged and mocked Ray's decision to build the baseball field. "This stupid baseball field's gonna bankrupt you," he says. Mark symbolizes the part of the psyche that internalizes the practical concerns of the outer world and opposes the inner work of the self. The conflict intensifies when Mark threatens to take over the farm. He warns Ray, "It's time to put away your little fantasy and come down to earth. We can't keep a useless baseball diamond in the middle of rich farmland." For Mark, the only measure of value is money, so the symbolic work of the baseball field is completely without value.

On the other side of the debate stand the archetypal figures of anima and wise old man who speak up in support of the value of inner work. Karin is the first to see and articulate the value in the field. "Daddy," his daughter assures him, "we don't have to sell the farm. People will come, from all over. They'll drive up and they'll want to pay us, like buying a ticket." Terrence picks up Karin's position and develops it further:

> People will come, Ray. They'll come to Iowa for reasons they can't even fathom. They'll turn up your driveway, not knowing for sure why they're doing it. They'll pass over the money without even thinking about it. For it is money they have and peace they lack. Oh, people will come, Ray. People will most definitely come.

Anima and wise old man affirm the unique value of symbolic work and contend that other people will recognize its value and be drawn to the peace it brings. People will even be willing to exchange money for the peace that flows from this healing, inner work.

Mark responds to Karin and Terrence by giving voice to a common fear that inhibits inner work. He counters, saying simply, "You will lose everything."

The conflict reaches a climax when Mark and Ray struggle over Karin and accidentally knock her off the bleachers. When Doc Graham comes off the field to save the little girl's life, Mark is finally able to see the baseball players and the value of the field. "Do not sell this farm, Ray," he says. Mark's transformation shows that, in the end, even the practical concerns of the psyche can be integrated into the work of the self.

What I recognized in this debate between Mark, Karin and Terrence was the internal conflict I felt as I struggled to decide whether to pursue the symbolic work of writing this book. Like Ray Kinsella, I felt pulled back and forth by competing voices that argued inside me. On one side, I heard a practical voice reminding me of my responsibilities to my family. On the other side, I heard a voice from deep within calling me to tell my father's story. The debate became particularly intense when I was trying to decide whether to quit my job so I would have more time for writing. *Field of Dreams* taught me to be patient with the internal conflict and trust that the healing inner work of the self would become so manifest that even the practical considerations of everyday life would be satisfied. If I remained faithful to the inner call of the self, even my practical concerns would be addressed through the healing process.

Having successfully resolved the tension between symbolic work and practical concerns, Ray Kinsella must confront one final issue before he is ready for the final act of reconciliation. When Ray hears that Terrence has been invited to join the other players in the tall corn, he jealously complains: "I have done everything I was told. I didn't understand but I did it. And I haven't once asked, 'What's in it for me?'" "So what are you saying, Ray?" Joe asks. Ray answers, "What's in it for me?" (This present question contrasts sharply with the earlier question that initiated Ray's symbolic work, "What do you want from me?")

What I heard in Ray's words was the voice of the ego complaining about all the work it had done and demanding some kind of recognition or gratification for itself. When the ego starts to connect to the energy flowing up from the deeper levels of the unconscious, there is a tendency on the part of the ego to want to claim this sense of power as its own rather than realizing that the power flows from the deeper self. Joe's response to Ray serves to remind the ego of its purpose. Joe says to Ray, "Is that why you did this, for you?" That is to say, were you working to satisfy a superficial ego need or were you working in response to the call of the self?

Ray wants to see what is in the cornfield, but Joe tells him he is not invited. Only Terrence is invited to enter the cornfield and the reason given is that he will write about what he finds there. Ray says, "I want a full description." Terrence responds, "Take care of this family." For me, this scene indicates that the ego resolves the issue by accepting a division of roles. The ego accepts responsibility for acting in the external world and leaves to the inner work of writing and storytelling the role of entering into the unconscious. Although the ego cannot enter directly into the unconscious, it can access the creative and healing energy of the unconscious through writing and storytelling. What I learned from this scene was to accept the responsibilities of everyday life and not look to my inner work for ego gratification, but be satisfied with whatever emerged from the writing and storytelling.

Because Ray Kinsella remains faithful to his inner work, he is now ready to receive the gift he has been working toward without realizing it—the opportunity to reconnect to his father. As Terrence disappears into the cornfield, Ray and Annie turn back toward Shoeless Joe who repeats the words that initiated Ray's quest. "If you build it, he will come," Joe says as he looks at the last player remaining on the field. Ray looks at the player and recognizes that it is his father. When Ray and Annie repeat the two subsequent messages that guided the quest ("Ease his pain." "Go the distance."), it is evident that all three instructions refer to this moment of revelation. At first, Ray presumes that the instructions came from Shoeless Joe, but Joe is quick to correct his misconception. "No, Ray, it was you," Joe says, revealing clearly it was Ray's own inner self that initiated and guided the symbolic work through the whole journey. By following the instructions coming from the unconscious, the conscious ego has allowed the father archetype to emerge into consciousness.

This was the scene that I both longed for and dreaded. The thought that I might someday see my father has been with me as long as I can remember. When I first saw the scene, it sent a shudder of pain and recognition through my heart. But then as I watched it over and over, it became a source of consolation and reassurance for me. This scene reassured me that, even though a father is dead, he can still appear in a way that is real and effective in its impact on the psyche. The doorway for his entrance is the dialogue between the conscious ego and the deeper self that is opened through inner work. I was now confident that, by attending to the messages coming from my inner self and following its instructions, I could open a doorway through which my father could truly enter my life.

After recognizing his father, Ray introduces him to his wife and daughter. Then Annie and Karin return to the house leaving Ray and his father on the baseball field. Father and son talk about heaven and dreams coming true. When it comes time to part, Ray and his father shake hands. Then John Kinsella starts walking toward the tall corn. Ray calls after his father with the words that complete his reconciliation, "Hey Dad, wanna have a catch?"

What I heard in Ray's words was a plea for forgiveness. The boy who once refused to have a catch with his father now says he is sorry and wants to reconnect. The father answers, "I'd like that." The father accepts the invitation thereby expressing his forgiveness. The son's symbolic work has made it possible for the father to appear and grant his forgiveness. Father and son reconnect and the split between ego and father archetype is healed.

Father and son then have a catch in the middle of the field. For me, the ball flying back and forth between Ray and his father represents the ego and father archetype reconnected in active dialogue. The split-off aspect of the self is reintegrated with the whole personality. More importantly, the father archetype functions as a stand-in for the deeper self in this scene. According to Edward Edinger, alienation between the ego and an archetype is ultimately alienation between the ego and the self.[36] I therefore see the catch between Ray and his father also as a symbol for a dialogue between the ego and the deeper self.

The final catch between Ray and his father represents what Edinger calls the ego-self axis.[37] The movement of the ball between father and son indicates that a healthy axis of communication has been established between ego and self. Ray and his father throwing a ball back and forth in the middle of the baseball field is a visual portrayal of an internal dialogue between ego and self taking place within the protected psychic space of a mandala. The inner conflict has been resolved. Ego and self are in active communication and the conscious personality is united to its deeper center. The ego has come home from the exile of being alienated from the self. By reconnecting to the father archetype, Ray has forged a deeper union with his inner self and to that degree his soul has been healed. The goal of this phase of individuation has been achieved.

As the camera lifts off the field, it reveals the baseball field illuminated in a circle of light and surrounded by darkness. An unending string of car lights zigzags across the darkened Iowa landscape working its way toward the light of the field. The scene reminds me of an inscription Jung carved in his mandala, the Tower. Next to the figure of a small man, an image of the self, Jung wrote, "[He] roams through the dark regions of this cosmos and glows like a star out of the depths. He points the way to the gates of the sun and to the land of dreams."[38] Ray Kinsella's "field of dreams" glows in the darkness and points the way to a process of healing and to a deeper psychic center that guides the journey to wholeness. What I see in the unending string of car lights is the longing of the human heart for this kind of healing. Others are drawn to Ray Kinsella's mandala because they find in his symbolic work a method for moving toward wholeness and peace.

This final scene of the movie taught me to trust that, if I do my inner work of healing, others might also benefit from what I learn. I have come therefore to understand my own inner work as a way of assisting in the healing of others.[39]

Field of Dreams suggests that, if we follow the call of the self and work to heal our own souls, we transform not only ourselves but also the world in which we live. The healing effect of inner work may even reach beyond the realm of this life. In their final conversation together, John Kinsella asks his son a question Shoeless Joe had asked earlier: "Is this heaven?" This time Ray does not say,

"No," but simply answers, "It's Iowa." John responds, "Could have sworn it was heaven." John's answer moves Ray to ask, "Is there a heaven?" Without a moment's hesitation, John replies, "Oh yeah, it's the place dreams come true." Ray looks toward the baseball field then up at the house where Annie and Karin are swinging on the porch and muses, "Maybe this is heaven." By building his baseball field, Ray Kinsella has moved beyond the limits of the earthly realm and into the realm of eternity.

For me, this scene implies that our symbolic work is actually heavenly work. When we allow the inner symbols and images arising from dreams to speak their truth in our conscious lives, we move toward a wholeness that is eternal. The distinction between conscious and unconscious is a condition of this life. When we die, the distinction will fall away. What remains is that wholeness, that third something that is fashioned through the dialogue between conscious and unconscious, what Jung calls the self. Symbolic work therefore heals the soul in preparation for its ultimate destiny. Following Ray Kinsella's story has given me further cause to hope that such a destiny is open to all of us.

3   First Steps

The Inner Journey

When I looked back over Ray Kinsella's story and the many ways in which it paralleled my own, I realized that the blueprint it provided actually laid out two pathways for me to follow in my journey to connect to my father: an inner path and an outer path. The inner journey, which I call soul work, involved introverted activities like writing and symbolic action to create an inner dialogue between the conscious ego and the deeper self. The outer journey involved extraverted activities like travelling and meeting people to expand and deepen the process of healing. This chapter recounts the steps of the inner journey; the following chapter covers the outer journey.

When I speak of the inner journey or soul work, I mean consciously and intentionally engaging the deeper self or soul by imaginatively working with symbols to access and channel the creative and healing energies of the unconscious. In *Field of Dreams*, I discovered a map for this inner journey, a model for the practice of soul work. The map laid out a five-step program of action:

1. Hearing the Call
2. Responding with Symbolic Action
3. Waiting Attentively
4. Circling Inward
5. Connecting to Ancestors

Soul work begins when one hears a mysterious call coming up from the deeper, unconscious layers of the psyche. One responds to the call through some action that consciously engages the images and symbols arising from the unconscious. There follows a period of attentive waiting that allows the unconscious freedom to do its work. Through a dynamic rhythm of acting and waiting, the conscious ego establishes a dialogue with the inner self. Once established, the dialogue is open to further development. One way to deepen the dialogue and thus advance the journey inward is by working with mandala symbols. Another way is by connecting to ancestors. Using this map takes one ever more deeply into the core of psychic life.

What follows is an account of my attempt to move along this inner path. At each step of the journey, I begin with an image from the movie. I then attempt to amplify the symbolic meaning of that image by referring to some text that resonates with the image. The resonant text intensifies and enriches the movie image, thereby clarifying its contribution to the inner journey. As St. Ignatius advises in the *Spiritual Exercises*, "[I]t is not much knowledge that fills and satisfies the soul, but the intimate understanding and relish of the truth."[1] Reflecting on a resonant text yields a more intimate understanding of the image and a deeper appreciation for its truth. Having thus amplified the meaning of the image, I then apply it to my journey to find my father.

Step One: Hearing the Call

Ray Kinsella's inner journey begins when he hears a faint, whisper-like voice. Barely audible at first, the voice becomes clearer with each repetition: "If you build it, he will come." This soft, gentle voice calling Ray to perform an important task reminded me of the "still small voice" in which the prophet Elijah encountered God:

> And behold, the Lord passed by, and a great and strong wind rent the mountains, and broke in pieces the rocks before the Lord, but the Lord was not in the wind; and after the wind an earthquake, but the Lord was not in the earthquake; and after the earthquake a fire, but the Lord was not in the fire; and after the fire a still small voice. And when Elijah heard it, he wrapped his face in his mantle and went out and stood at the entrance of the cave. And behold, there came a voice to him, and said, "What are you doing here, Elijah?"(1 Kings 19:11-13, RSV)

The call of Elijah has always been one of my favorite biblical stories because it speaks to me of the gentle, almost imperceptible, way in which God communicates with us. It reassures me to know that God is to be found not in extraordinary events but in the quiet, ordinary moments of our everyday lives.

When I first noticed a similarity between the appearance of the voice in *Field of Dreams* and the call of the prophet Elijah, I was intrigued by the possibility that Ray Kinsella's call might be following the pattern of a biblical call narrative, a story about someone being called by God for a special mission. I did not have to go very far to confirm my thesis. Right after Ray hears the mysterious voice for the first time, he walks into the house and takes off his shoes. This simple act of a farmer who has been working out in the fields acquires new meaning when it is viewed in the context of a biblical call narrative. When God calls to Moses from the burning bush, he says, "Put off your shoes from your feet, for the place on which you are standing is holy ground"(Exodus 3:5). Ray Kinsella's call also resembles the call of Moses in that the call establishes a link to the father. Moses is told, "I am the God of your father. The God of Abraham, the God of Isaac, and the God of Jacob"(Exodus 3:6).

If I had any remaining doubts about the parallels between a biblical call narrative and Ray Kinsella's call, the doubts were completely dispelled when I turned to the call of the prophet Ezekiel. In the story of Ezekiel's call the prophet has a vision. Ezekiel sees "four living creatures" in "the form of men, but each had four faces," "the face of a man in front," "the face of a lion on the right side," "the face of an ox on the left side," and "the face of an eagle at the back"(Ezekiel 1:1-14). Beside the living creatures were four wheels, one for each creature.

> As for the appearance of the wheels and their construction: their appearance was like the gleaming of a chrysolite; and the four had the same likeness, their construction being as it were a wheel within a wheel. And when the living creatures went, the wheels went beside them; for the spirit of the living creatures was in the wheels.(Ezekiel 1:15-20)

Ezekiel's vision is fascinating because of its mandala-like qualities: wheels spinning within wheels enveloping four creatures each with four faces. Moreover, the four faces constitute a quaternity that follows the pattern of three plus one: four elements in which three are similar and a fourth is somehow unique or special. In Ezekiel's vision, there are three animal faces (lion, ox, and eagle) and a fourth human face. Like Ezekiel, Ray Kinsella also receives a mandala-like vision: a four-sided baseball field in which three elements (first, second and third bases) are similar and a fourth is somehow unique or special (home plate).

It seems clear that, intentionally or not, the call of Ray Kinsella conforms to the pattern of a biblical call narrative. What does this amplified image of call tell me about the practice of soul work?

First of all, it tells me to be attentive to the possibility of a call. The call need not be an extraordinary experience but simply an awareness that I am being addressed from somewhere deep within. It is a call from the deeper self. It tells me that my conscious ego is not alone. It has a companion. My inner life is not a monologue but a dialogue. And by engaging in this dialogue, I can move toward greater psychological health and wholeness.

The experience of hearing a call is an archetypal pattern that reveals the dialogue nature of our inner lives. In a biblical context, the dialogue is framed as a conversation between the individual and God. In a Jungian context, while not excluding the possibility of a conversation with God, the dialogue is framed in terms of an interior communication between the conscious ego and the deeper self. Whether one chooses to hear the voice of God in the call of the deeper self is a matter of personal faith. In my own experience, it is helpful to understand the inner dialogue as ultimately a dialogue with God, or whatever name one associates with the Higher Power of the Universe. But whether the call comes from God or the deeper self, the experience of a call is not something rare and reserved for exceptional individuals. Interior dialogue is a universal pattern that invites a person into a process of inner transformation and healing.

An important step on the path of soul work was therefore to broaden my understanding of personal identity beyond the limits of a narrowly defined ego that fancies itself the center of all experience and the source of all knowledge and action. My true identity is fashioned by an interior dialogue in which the conscious ego is an essential but limited partner. The other partner in this dialogue is a deeper self, a deeper wisdom that guides and directs my on-going development as a person.

One of the clearest ways that I become aware of the inner dialogue between ego and self is when I find myself addressed by an inner voice that is clearly distinct from the "I" presently organizing and directing my life. The beginning of the dialogue may be as simple as a "still small voice" that tells me something is lacking in my life, something is missing that demands attention. It can begin with a quiet, almost indiscernible, prompting to do something not as yet defined.

Furthermore, when I hear this voice, I am on holy ground. For me, it is holy ground because ultimately the call is an encounter with God, but even if I do not hear this voice as the voice of God, still the call is an encounter with transcendence. When I am addressed by an inner voice that speaks to me from my depths, I am on holy ground because I am engaged in dialogue with that mysterious center of psychic life that transcends the limits of the conscious ego.

Once I sense I am being addressed, no matter how faint the call, the next important step is to actively listen to whatever is calling for my attention. Because this is a personal encounter with mystery, the proper attitude is one of reverence and attention. Ray Kinsella's simple response, "Who are you? What do you want from me?" marked a significant turning point in the progress of his healing. I have to assume a comparable attitude of openness indicating my willingness to listen and respond. By assuming such an attitude, I recognize the truth that I am being called and I prepare myself to receive some answer.

How has this amplified image of call functioned in my journey to connect to my father? I believe I received a call when I first viewed the movie, *Field of Dreams*. The emotional impact of the movie told me that I needed to do something to try to connect to my father, but at first it was not clear what I should do. I considered going to the Marine Corps Archives in Suitland, Maryland to research my father's military career. I also imagined going to Saipan to visit the place where he was killed. But neither of these possibilities developed beyond the idea stage. Gradually, I realized that the voice was calling me to write a book about my search for my father. It felt as though I were listening to an inner conversation:

If you write, he will come.
What shall I write?
Stay faithful to the task and it will be given to you.

This project has now taken me far beyond where I ever imagined I could go. All along the way, the inner voice has been guiding me and gradually clarifying what I should do. At times it seemed as though I was wandering aimlessly because I could not find the path to follow. Now I realize that the inner journey does not follow a clearly laid out formula like a well-constructed symphony, but is rather more like a classic jazz composition in which themes are developed through a pattern of "call and response" among the various instruments. What has finally emerged in my efforts to follow this pattern of "call and response" has completely exceeded my original expectations in fulfilling the deepest longing of my soul.

Step Two: Responding with Symbolic Action

In *Field of Dreams*, Ray Kinsella responds to the call of the self by building the baseball field. The baseball field becomes the operative symbol for his inner work. The symbol of the baseball field acts as a channel for communication between the conscious ego and the deeper self. The unconscious spontaneously produces the symbol of the baseball field thereby opening a channel through which the ego can respond. By actually building the baseball field, the conscious ego in effect says to the unconscious, "I have heard the call of the self and I want to engage in a dialogue by responding through this symbol."

The physical work of building the baseball field is an exercise of active imagination, a way of consciously interacting with a symbol arising from the unconscious. As the term "active imagination" implies, conscious engagement with symbols requires some action. The action may be as simple as concentrating on a mental picture, but to further strengthen the connection between the conscious ego and the unconscious, nothing is quite as effective as participating in some concrete, physical activity. Since we are embodied psyches, the use of the body in symbolic action has a way of deepening our sense of wholeness.

In *Field of Dreams*, the physical action is emphasized by the way the camera continually focuses the viewer's attention on the physical details of building the field: mowing down the corn; plowing, raking and rolling the field; driving a nail into the wood of the bleachers. When I watched the way Ray Kinsella responded to his call by building the baseball field, I wondered whether the work of writing would be physical enough to qualify as a comparable symbolic action. Then I recalled a poem of Seamus Heaney that unites the symbolic action of writing with the physical labor of digging. This poem amplified the image of building the baseball field in such a way that I was able to apply it more aptly to my own soul work.

Digging

Between my finger and my thumb
The squat pen rests; snug as a gun.

Under my window, a clean rasping sound
When the spade sinks into gravelly ground:
My father, digging. I look down

Till his straining rump among the flowerbeds

Bends low, comes up twenty years away
Stooping in rhythm through potato drills
Where he was digging.

The course boot nestled on the lug, the shaft
Against the inside knee was levered firmly.
He rooted out tall tops, buried the bright edge deep
to scatter new potatoes that we picked
Loving their cool hardness in our hands.

By God, the old man could handle a spade.
Just like his old man.

My grandfather cut more turf in a day
Than any other man on Toner's bog.

Once I carried him milk in a bottle
Corked sloppily with paper. He straightened up
To drink it, then fell to right away
Nicking and slicing neatly, heaving sods
Over his shoulder, going down and down
For the good turf. Digging.

The cold smell of potato mould, the squelch and slap
Of soggy peat, the curt cuts of an edge
Through living roots awaken in my head.
But I've no spade to follow men like them.

Between my finger and my thumb
The squat pen rests.
I'll dig with it.[2]

The poet is holding his pen, preparing to write. He hears his father outside digging in the flowerbeds. He looks out the window and watches his father until the scene triggers a memory of digging for potatoes with his father twenty years earlier. This recollection triggers another memory in which the poet recalls watching his grandfather digging turf. The image of digging leads him to remember the work of his father and grandfather with affection and admiration. Similar to the camera in *Field of Dreams*, the poet focuses the reader's attention on the physical details of their labors: the course boot nestled on the lug; the shaft against the inside knee; digging, straining, stooping; nicking, slicing, heaving. Then the poet reflects on his own work and realizes that it too is a form of digging. Like a spade, the pen is a tool, but a tool for symbolic work, revealing the deeper meaning in simple, commonplace actions like digging in a garden or cutting turf. The pen too is a tool for "going down and down for the good turf." Through this insight, the poet realizes that his work is united to the work of his father and grandfather, thus creating a bond between the generations.

Reading Heaney's poem and feeling the "squat pen" in my hand helps me to appreciate the physical action and symbolic power of writing. The poem amplifies the movie image in such a way that I can see the work of writing as a symbolic action comparable to building a baseball field. Writing about my father is the shape of my symbolic action, my response to a call, "going down and down" to the deeper layers of the self "for the good turf" that heals the soul. Just as Ray Kinsella connects to his father through building the baseball field and Seamus Heaney connects to his father and grandfather through writing poetry, my soul work is to find my father by writing this book and telling his story.

Step Three: Waiting Attentively

After Ray Kinsella builds the baseball field, he enters a period of attentive waiting. He sits patiently watching his field through the rhythm of day and night and the change of seasons. "Something's gonna happen out there; I can feel it," he says confidently. Symbolic action requires some activity, but then there follows a necessary contemplative phase in which the conscious ego suspends its activity and allows the unconscious freedom to act. Doing something is only the first phase of symbolic action. There is a corresponding need for receptivity, an openness to receive whatever the unconscious produces in response to the symbolic action.

Ray Kinsella's attentive watching of his baseball field provided an image that encouraged me to be patient and open in my soul work and to trust in the slow working of the inner process. Then I remembered a letter that amplified the image of Ray's attentive waiting. The letter was written by Teilhard de Chardin, a Jesuit priest, scientist, and mystic. While serving as a stretcher-bearer in the French army during World War I, Teilhard wrote to his cousin, Marguerite Teillard-Chambon:

> Above all, trust in the slow work of God. We are, quite naturally, impatient in everything to reach the end without delay. We should like to skip the intermediate stages. We are impatient of being on the way to something unknown, something new. And yet it is the law of all progress that it is made by passing through some stages of instability—and that may take a very long time.
>
> And so, I think, it is with you. Your ideas mature gradually—let them grow, let them shape themselves, without undue haste. Don't try to 'force' them on, as though you could be today what time (that is to say, grace and circumstances acting on your own good will) will make you tomorrow.

As I reflected on Teilhard's words, it felt as though my father was addressing them to me: "Trust in the slow work of God. Your ideas mature gradually. Let them grow. Let them shape themselves. Don't try to force them on." Words of comfort from a World War I stretcher-bearer to a young cousin became the words of a World War II Marine encouraging his son to be patient with the slow work of writing and healing. Whenever I became discouraged by the slow progress of my work, I would read these words and picture Ray Kinsella sitting alone at a frosted windowpane, watching his baseball field fill with snow. Even the softly falling snowflakes spoke to me of the quiet, barely discernible movement of the unconscious that accompanies our inner work and the gentle action of God's grace in the depths of our souls.

Gradually, I discovered that attentive waiting might include activity that does not require much conscious attention. Slow rhythmic activities like swimming or walking became occasions in which a word or phrase would come to me, particularly when my writing felt blocked at the level of conscious effort. Because I never knew when something might surface, I learned to keep some writing materials always close at hand. As long as I remained faithful to the symbolic action of writing, the unconscious would not fail to do its part.

Step Four: Circling Inward

In *Field of Dreams*, the symbolic action revolves around the symbolism of a mandala. Not only is the baseball field shaped like a mandala (a radial arrangement emanating from a central point and containing a four-sided square), but the ultimate goal of the game also follows a mandala pattern (circling around the bases and returning home). In Jungian terms, circling a four-sided baseball diamond would be described as a circumambulation of a mandala. The mandala provides an archetypal pattern for inner work, a map to facilitate one's journey to the center of psychic life. For Ray Kinsella, the inner journey resulted in an encounter with his father and a dialogue with his own deeper self.

For me, a "text" that amplified the mandala symbol of the baseball field was the design of a labyrinth that was placed in the floor of Chartres Cathedral around the year 1220. A labyrinth is one particular form in which the more general mandala pattern may appear. The labyrinth of Chartres is a circular figure containing a complex winding map that leads one from the exterior of the figure to its inner core. The pathway follows a single course winding back and forth through the four quadrants of the mandala pattern. Unlike a maze, there are no alternative pathways and no dead ends in a labyrinth.

The purpose of the labyrinth is to provide a unique space within which to perform a walking meditation. One enters the labyrinth from the outside and follows the winding pathway inward through the four quadrants, slowly spiraling toward the center. When one arrives at the center of the labyrinth, there is a flower-shaped space where one can pause and pray, allowing the experience of being centered to deepen. When one is ready, one follows the same convoluted path on a return journey from the center back to the labyrinth's outer rim.

The labyrinth offers the body and the psyche a distinct way of moving inward to a core of inner space and then moving outward along the same clear path to an external realm. By so doing, it expresses with physical movement the inner psychic movement from the external concerns of ego-consciousness to the inner core of the self and the return journey to the external world with a deeper sense of being centered. The physical pathway of the labyrinth is a mirror of the soul's inner journey into wholeness, a wholeness that comes from being unified and centered. By physically moving in this mandala pattern, body and psyche work together to achieve a deeper level of integration between conscious and unconscious dimensions of the psyche.

Since the labyrinth mirrors one's inner journey to wholeness, meditatively walking this pathway can release unconscious feelings of joy and sorrow that are not immediately available to consciousness. Issues that otherwise might remain buried in the unconscious may come to the surface for conscious attention.

My experience of the labyrinth began unwittingly several years back when Michelle and I visited Chartres Cathedral. Even before we reached the cathedral, I was enchanted by the place. It felt as though the building was drawing me through the narrow streets of the town and up the hill from which the magnificent edifice rises. When we entered the building, the rich color and intricate detail of the stained glass windows captivated me. As I walked slowly around the building from window to window, I concentrated on the vivid colors and the stories they told, but it felt like the building was calling to me on a deeper level that I could not quite understand. Even after I studied each window in detail, I wanted to continue wandering around the building as though I was looking for something that I could not quite fathom.

At the time I was completely ignorant of mandalas. I never even noticed the labyrinth on the nave floor because it was almost completely covered by chairs arranged for a Eucharistic liturgy. Something in the building was holding my unconscious attention and it would not let me go. Just moving around within the sacred space of the cathedral seemed to satisfy some longing in my soul, but I could not figure out how or why. I circled the building several times, both inside and outside. Even after we left the building, I lay in quiet contemplation on a hotel bed looking out through the opened balcony doors toward the spires of the cathedral towering above me, still in the grip of the mysterious structure.

A few years after our visit to Chartres, I discovered the source of my unusual experience. I was just starting to write about *Field of Dreams* when I attended a Jungian conference at an Episcopal retreat house in North Carolina. In one of the conference workshops, a canvas replica of the Chartres labyrinth was laid out on the floor of a large meeting hall. When I read a description of the labyrinth's purpose, I realized that I had actually been circling the labyrinth while I walked around Chartres Cathedral. I wondered whether the strange attraction I felt while walking around the cathedral was an invitation to enter into the labyrinth. Recalling my experience at Chartres, I decided to respond to the invitation by making a walking meditation on the canvas labyrinth.

On two successive days, I made a 45-minute walking meditation within the labyrinth. As I followed the pathway to the center, Gregorian chant played in the background supporting an atmosphere of medieval prayer and recollection. On each occasion, I exited the labyrinth with a gentle feeling of calm and peace.

On the third day, I reentered the labyrinth for another walking meditation. As I was leaving the inner core for my return journey outward, I found myself thinking about my mother and her difficulties with the early stages of Alzheimer's disease. As I thought about my mother a deep sense of sadness started to well up inside of me. My thoughts about my mother have usually been happy ones. My mother symbolizes all the security and love I knew as a child. It was her love and that of my grandparents that provided the safe container within which I was able to weather the loss of my father. But now I was feeling for my mother the kind of deep sadness that I usually experienced only in those rare moments when I allowed myself to feel the sorrow of my father's absence.

Some of my sadness came from realizing the suffering my mother would encounter as she moved through the various stages of this cruel disease. But in a surprising and remarkable way, it also felt as though I was feeling my father's sadness as he experienced my mother's illness. I could feel inside of me my father's abiding love and solicitude for the once-young bride he left so long ago.

Within the labyrinth experience, I realized that my father and I were joined together in our concern for my mother. Although the sorrow remained, I felt something shift inside. Confident that my father was still watching over my mother, I entrusted her to his care and accepted my part in looking after her. Without losing the feeling of sadness, I also sensed a deeper trust rising up to comfort me on my return journey through the labyrinth to the outer world.

Up to this time, I was not even aware of the inner trauma occasioned in me by my mother's illness. From my circling inward through the mandala pattern of the labyrinth, an area of psychic suffering had surfaced in my awareness and healing had begun. More importantly, the key to the healing was the experience of my father's presence. My experience in the labyrinth gave me a clear but fleeting hint that my father's spirit was stirring inside of me, that he was somehow available to me for the inner work I had yet to do.

Step Five: Connecting to Ancestors

Field of Dreams opens with a series of photographs showing Ray's father, John Kinsella, at various stages of his life. In the middle of this series, there is a photograph of John Kinsella in a baseball uniform looking over his left shoulder and clutching a catcher's mask to his chest. The photograph is significant because it shows precisely how John Kinsella will look at the end of the movie when he finally appears and is recognized by his son.

When Ray first notices his father, John Kinsella is bending over taking off his catcher's equipment. Then, the father rises slowly, turning toward his son while lifting the catcher's mask to his chest. As John Kinsella looks across the baseball field toward his son, he assumes exactly the same pose he held in the old photograph. When Ray sees his father in this position, he exclaims, "Oh my God! It's my father." The camera cuts back to John Kinsella, still clutching his catcher's mask to his chest and looking over his shoulder toward his son.

The scene suggests that the father's image has come alive through the son's contemplation of his father's photographs. John Kinsella appears with all the vitality of a young man. The barriers of time and death are overcome and Ray is finally able to connect to his father. As father and son gaze at each other across the green grass of the field, one can almost feel the power of the connection between them. The scene is particularly effective because it ties together the movie's opening photographic collage and the climatic moment when father and son are finally reunited, thereby highlighting the unity of the whole process of inner work that culminates in this moment of reunion.

John Kinsella walks slowly across the field toward Ray and his family. Father and son shake hands. Ray then says to his daughter, "Karin, this is my ..." He can't bring himself to say the word "father." So he stops short and begins again, "This is John." As they talk, father and son continue to gaze at each other. Annie and Karin excuse themselves, leaving Ray and his father alone to talk. Their conversation focuses on the nature of heaven. When they are about to part, father and son shake hands once again. As the camera focuses on their hands, the intensity of their grip becomes apparent. "Union" and "bonding" are the feelings that the image evokes. Then John turns and starts walking back toward the cornfield. With tears in his voice, Ray calls after him, "Hey, Dad, wanna have a catch?" "I'd like that," his father answers with the same tearful emotion rising in his words.

As I watched Ray Kinsella reunited with his father, I could feel a deep longing within me to somehow connect to my father. Then, I recalled a passage from Vergil that closely parallels the scene of Ray's reunion with his father. The passage, which tells the story of Aeneas meeting his father, Anchises, on the Fields of Elysium, provided me an ideal way to amplify the image of Ray Kinsella meeting his father in the field of dreams.

In Book VI of the *Aeneid*, Vergil describes how Aeneas, after his long journey following the Trojan Wars, arrives on the shores of Italy and descends into the Underworld, the abode of the dead. Guided by the Cumaean Sibyl, Aeneas comes eventually to the Elysian Fields, the final resting-place for the heroes of old and the souls of the blessed.

Vergil's description of the scene on the Fields of Elysium is almost a perfect replica of Ray's field of dreams:

> And so they came to the happy places,
> The pleasant green of the Fortunate Grove
> Where the blest dwell. The air is freer
> And dresses all the fields with brilliant light;
> They have their own sun, their own stars.
> Some exercise upon a playing field
> —Games on the grass or wrestling on yellow sand;

> A handsome lot, heroes in the great style
> And born in happier years, Ilus, Assarcus
> And Dardanus himself, who founded Troy.
> Aeneas sees others to left and right
> Taking a meal upon the grass, or singing
> A hymn of praise in chorus, in a grove
> of scented bay.[4]

Just as in *Field of Dreams*, the heroes of old play games under the bright lights and people take an evening meal on the green grass. When father and son finally meet, the details and dramatic tone in the *Aeneid* are almost identical to those in *Field of Dreams*:

> When he saw Aeneas
> Coming over the grass in his direction,
> Anchises stretched out both his hands eagerly,
> Tears started on his cheeks, he cried out:
> You have come at last, and filial devotion
> Has found the hard way as I knew it would.
> I am permitted, son, to see your face,
> Hear the familiar voice and talk with you!
> Aeneas answered:
> "It was your image, father, your sad image,
> So often seen, that brought me to these limits.
> Give me your right hand, father, give and do not
> Now slip from my embrace!"[5]

Here is the same tearful embrace of father and son, an embrace that comes after a long journey inspired and guided by the image of a father who has died. Just as the image of his father leads Aeneas to Anchises, so too the photographic image of John Kinsella nurtures Ray's active imagination and guides his inner journey of reconciliation with his father. The image of the father acts as a guide inviting the son to pursue a path that leads to reunion.

In both scenes, father and son stretch out toward each other expressing the desire of the generations to be reunited. Father yearns for union with the son as much as son longs for the father's embrace. And in both accounts the intensity of the embrace is palpable. As the camera focuses on the hands of Ray and John Kinsella locked in an intense grip, I can hear Aeneas' words: "Give me your right hand, father, and do not now slip from my embrace!" Imaginatively entering into the scene, I experience the yearning of mortals down through the ages to remain connected to those from whom they receive life and those to whom they give life.

The parallels between *Field of Dreams* and the *Aeneid* continue. Once father and son are reunited, the conversation turns quickly to a discussion of the afterlife offering the father an opportunity to answer the son's questions about the relationship between this world and the next. Anchises goes into a detailed explanation of the transmigration of souls from one body to another. Ray Kinsella asks, "Is there a heaven?" His father answers, "Oh yeah, it's the place dreams come true." Ray's response is, "Maybe this is heaven."

Each father in his own way shares with his son the wisdom that comes from beyond the grave and the message is similar: this world and the next are more closely woven together than usually imagined. The separation between these two realms is less real than the continuity between them. Therefore, the longing of the human heart for connection between the generations is not a futile yearning based on illusion, but a consoling truth grounded in reality.

Two thousand years of literature and history separate Virgil's epic poem from the movie *Field of Dreams*, but both offer the same message. The image of ancestor and descendant straining toward each other is an archetypal image rooted in the structure of the psyche expressing the yearning of the generations for union. The two scenes of reunion between father and son capture the universal longing of the generations to overcome the barriers of time and death and be reunited. The generations seem to reach out toward each other across the boundary between this life and the next. The reaching moves in both directions: the living toward the dead and the dead toward the living, son reaching toward father and father reaching toward son. There is a bond between the generations that is not broken by death.

Inspired by the scenes of Ray Kinsella and Aeneas reunited with their fathers, I decided to follow my own path of "filial devotion" and apply this amplified image to my search for my father. I began by collecting photographs of my father and arranging them around me on the desk and bookshelves in the room where I write. Several photographs show my father in his dress green lieutenant's uniform. As I carefully studied these photographs, I recalled that once, years before, I had seen a similar uniform in an old trunk in my mother's cellar.

On my next visit to my mother's house, I went looking for that old trunk. I climbed down the crumbling cement steps of the cellar, remembering to duck my head as I passed under the low hanging water pipes. Recognizing the damp, dusty smell of the cellar, I recalled a dream Jung once had about descending into the lower levels of a cellar. For Jung, the dream marked his discovery of the deeper, collective levels of the unconscious.[6] As I looked about me, I secretly hoped that this descent into the cellar of my childhood might also occasion some valuable discovery.

A wood slatted door sealed off the section of the cellar where my Italian grandmother used to store her homemade tomato sauce and hang her rainy day laundry. The smell of cooking tomatoes and freshly cleaned linens floated through my memory. The door was hanging from one hinge so I lifted it gently with both hands and rested it against the cement wall.

Inside the storage cellar, I saw several blankets covering a large object in the middle of the floor. I pulled back the blankets and found underneath a dried-out plastic table cloth now permanently molded into the shape of the object it covered. Under the table cloth was an old wooden steamer trunk. As I raised the lid of the trunk, I saw a bundle wrapped with a yellowed bed sheet. Pinned to the sheet was an envelope with the words, "La vesta di sposa di Palma," written in my grandmother's handwriting. It was my mother's wedding dress. My grandmother had carefully put it away, marking it as Palma's wedding dress. I opened the package just enough to recognize the fabric of the dress my mother was wearing in the wedding portrait that hangs on our dining room wall.

Underneath the wedding dress was another bundle wrapped in a clear plastic dry-cleaning bag. Through the plastic I could see the unmistakable dark green of a Marine Corps uniform. My grandmother had discreetly put away my father's uniform with my mother's wedding dress. My grandmother's thoughtfulness in preserving my parents' wedding garments brought to mind the warmth and intimacy that characterized the sixty years she and my mother lived together.

I took the green bundle out of the trunk, but I resisted opening it. It did not seem to be the appropriate time or place. I left the wedding dress in the trunk as I had found it. This was still my mother's home. Although I knew she would not want to see the dress, it was still her dress and it belonged with her. But my father's uniform now belonged with me. It was time for me to bring it to my home. I put the uniform in the back of my car and drove the seven hours back to Virginia.

That night I brought the still unopened bundle to the room where I had arranged my father's photographs. I lay the bundle on the floor and opened it carefully. There was a sense of mystery as I approached this package from the past. Opening it seemed to evoke the kind of awe and respect usually associated with sacred ritual. It was only a bundle of clothes, but for me it was a messenger from another realm. I wondered whether my father might have left something in a pocket, something that would be a message to me from beyond the grave.

The first item I examined was a wool garrison cap with the familiar Marine insignia of globe and anchor. I looked inside the cap. On the leather headband was stamped the name, "A T MOORE." As I held the cap I pictured it resting on my father's head. The headband was clearly worn from perspiration. I ran my finger over the leather headband, aware that I was actually touching the traces of my father's sweat.

When I pulled out the next item, I was surprised to find a uniform jacket with a complete set of insignia: globe and anchor on the lapel pins and first lieutenant's bars on the epaulets. This was the very same jacket my father was wearing in several of the photographs I had arranged on my desk. The jacket was in nearly perfect condition with barely a wrinkle. Even the silver bars were still shining. It looked as though my father had taken the uniform off just the day before, rather than fifty years earlier.

Touching the heavy wool-serge fabric made my father seem so close, so immediate, so real. As I held the silver bars between my fingers, I could feel him pinning them on the jacket. It was as though time stood still for a moment and I was back in the past with my father as he prepared to put on his uniform. 1944 did not seem so far away. I was somehow meeting my father in a "now" that had neither past nor future.

Bringing my father's uniform up from the dark, musty graveyard of my mother's cellar lifted my father up from the darker recesses of my unconscious. Placing his uniform in the room with his photographs brought him into the light of my conscious awareness. I could feel his presence with a freshness and immediacy that is difficult to explain. As I held his photograph, looked into his smiling eyes and touched the jacket he was wearing in the photograph, it was as though he was actually in the room with me. Just as my clothes are a part of me, so his clothing felt like his presence in this world. Somehow, through the symbolic action of combining imagination with the physical senses of touch and sight, I had established a bridge between this world and the next. My father and I were no longer separated by time and death. I experienced, if only for a moment, my father's touch.

A few weeks after this experience, I was driving back to Washington from Richmond, Virginia on Interstate 95. As I approached the exit for Quantico Marine Base, something inside told me to take the turn-off. My father had done his officer's training at Quantico, so I decided to follow the impulse, not knowing what to expect.

Once on the base, I followed the signs for the Officer Candidate School. I wasn't sure how much the place might have changed over time, but something was encouraging me to move forward. When I got to the area of the Officer Candidate School, I found one large building that looked old enough to have been there in the '40s. I parked behind the building and walked around to the front. The building faced east toward the Potomac River. It was a bright sunny fall afternoon. As I walked south along the front of the building, the sun was just beginning to move behind it. I was walking in the sun with the Potomac River on my left and the old building on my right. I wondered whether this cement walkway was where my father had walked. Then, just as I crossed from the warmth of the sunshine into the cool shade of the building, it was as though the building reached out and touched me, ever so gently. It felt as though all the years of the building's history were washing over me. The past no longer felt like the past but rather like a part of the present. I knew in that moment that this must be the place where my father had lived.

I went inside the building and walked around, trying to get a deeper sense of the place. Temporary dry wall obscured the building's original floor plan, but in the stairwell the mahogany railings and worn steps appeared the way they might have looked when my father climbed those stairs. I went back outside and stared at the Greek revival archway, fixing the details of the building in my mind.

As soon as I got home, I pulled out the yearbook of my father's graduation class from Officer Candidate School. There under the caption, "Reserve Officers' Barracks," was a picture of the building I had just visited. The photograph confirmed my presentiment that I had found my father's barracks. It felt like I had stepped back in time.

In my trip to Quantico, I journeyed back to the '40s, just as I had when I held my father's uniform. These two brief encounters gave me a taste of what might be possible in connecting to my father, a taste that invited me to move forward on my journey. I was beginning to trust that there was a realm beyond the barriers of time and death where my father and I could meet.

Later, I found a reference in Jung that illuminated the meaning of my experience. In certain aboriginal societies of Australia, the word "dreamtime" (aljira) refers to a timeless realm, a "ghostland," "in which the ancestors lived and still live."[7] According to this ancient cosmology, the world of dreams (i.e., the world of the unconscious) and the world of the ancestors are one. When I framed my experience in the light of this cosmology, I understood more clearly how the feeling of my father's "ghostly" presence could flow from my inner work. By establishing a dialogue with the unconscious through symbolic action, I had entered into the timeless "ghostland" where "the ancestors lived and still live." There, I encountered my father and felt his healing touch.

These intimations of my father's presence convinced me that he had a vested interest in the success of my inner work and that the fulfillment of my task depended on strengthening the connection to him. I have often felt that I was under the influence of issues and questions that were left unanswered by my father's early death at the age of twenty-three, that I had to complete something that was left unfinished by him. My personal destiny was to somehow continue the story that ended so abruptly on the night of June 15, 1944. Through my inner work, I was beginning to learn how my father was guiding me in the fulfillment of that destiny.

The practice of soul work had opened a doorway through which my father's healing presence could enter my life. In addition, this fifth step along the inner path—Connecting to Ancestors—had also included physical travel—to my mother's basement and my father's barracks—and therefore provided a fitting transition to the outer journey of the next chapter.

4   Pressing On

The External Journey

In *Field of Dreams*, Ray's initial work within the symbolic space of the mandala results in his receiving a second message. Just as he is getting comfortable with the symbolic action surrounding the baseball field, the voice returns and tells him, "Ease his pain." Ray understands the message to mean that he must go to Boston, Massachusetts to find Terrence Mann. From there, the voice sends him to Chisolm, Minnesota in search of Moonlight Graham. Along the way, these two companions provide wisdom and guidance for Ray's ongoing journey of healing. Ultimately, Ray returns home to the realm of inner work, the baseball field, where he finally finds his father.

What I saw in Ray's external journey was a movement outward from an interior world of mandala symbolism and active imagination to an expanded, exterior realm of symbolic action—a pilgrimage. Just as the baseball field provided a protective space for symbolic action, so too the symbolic external journey, the pilgrimage, became a container for a continuing process of inner healing and discovery.

Like Ray Kinsella, I found that the inner journey triggered an external journey, one that continued and deepened the process of inner healing and brought me closer to my father. The external journey flowed directly from the inner work. The initial stages of my inner work focused primarily on writing about *Field of Dreams*, Jung, and my father. Often, when I had a chance to express these ideas, people would come forward to share some personal anecdote connected to the movie or to my story. On one such occasion, I heard a "voice" in the words of one of the participants. At the end of a workshop I gave in Chicago, a woman handed me a slip of paper and said, "I have a friend you should meet. His father was also killed in World War II. I think the two of you are on the same journey. Here's his name and phone number." She seemed reluctant to talk further. Having delivered her message, she was ready to move on. It was a bit uncanny the way she appeared and disappeared so quickly.

With that brief encounter began a series of messages, delivered by a variety of guides and wisdom figures. These messages would lead me on a journey of discovery far beyond what I could ever have foreseen. My soul work and my search for my father shifted onto a pathway that seemed to be guided by unseen forces. As I followed this path I learned how to listen and respond. Soul work became less a task to be performed and more a gift to be received.

When I returned home from Chicago, I waited a few days before calling the number the woman had given me. I wasn't sure how much I wanted to go into all this "father stuff" with a total stranger. So, I just left the slip of paper on my desktop. Finally, on an impulse in the middle of a busy workday, I picked up the phone and dialed the number. I was a little surprised when Ken Green answered the phone—no answering machine or receptionist to give me time to prepare myself. I identified myself and tried to explain why I was calling. "Your friend suggested I give you a call," I told Ken, "I'm not really sure what to say except my father was a Marine who was killed in the Pacific."

Ken's father, a cavalry officer, was killed in Europe. Ken recounted how he had been trying for the last few years to learn more about his father and how he died. Ken's mother had saved all of her husband's letters. Ken had begun reading through the letters and typing them into his computer. He wasn't sure what he would do with the letters, but he was aware that reading and typing them was helping him connect to his father. He also told me that he kept a pair of his father's cavalry boots in his office. When he mentioned the boots, I told him about my father's uniform hanging in my room.

Just talking to Ken about our common experience stirred something deep inside of me. I started to fill up. My emotional reaction embarrassed me a little, but it was comforting to know that I was not alone in my loss or in the way I responded to it.

Ken also gave me a tip that would send my journey in a completely new direction. He mentioned that a network of World War II orphans had recently been formed and that they had helped him to find information about his father's service record. He gave me the name and phone number of a woman in Bellingham, Washington who was acting as a clearinghouse for the network. A few days later I called Ann Bennett Mix. She told me there were more than 900 people just like me, sons and daughters who were trying to learn more about their fathers who were killed in World War II. She also gave me the address of an organization in Alexandria, Virginia that maintained a current list of World War II veterans' reunions.

I had been planning to make a visit to the Marine Corps archives in Suitland, Maryland so I could get some information about my father's unit. I wanted to get as close as I could to him at the moment of death. Exactly how did he die? Where was he? What was he doing? What were his thoughts and feelings? What killed him? These were questions that had surfaced often over the years, but now they were coming forward in a way that demanded some action on my part. I thought that if only I could get some concrete details about the final days and moments of his life, I could somehow be present to him as he lay dying. The Marine Corps archives had seemed like a logical starting point, but now for the first time I realized that I might actually be able to contact someone who knew my father and served with him. So I sent the details of my father's unit, a dollar and a self-addressed envelope to Service Reunions.

Two weeks later, I received the name and phone number of a contact person for the Fourth Marine Division Association. I immediately called Fred Everett in Kissimmee, Florida and learned that members of the Fourth Marine Division had been meeting annually since 1947. Although they were originally formed to assist the children of deceased members, I had never even heard of them. Fred offered to send me a list of men who had served in my father's company. He also mentioned that there was going to be a dedication ceremony for a new monument honoring the members of the Fourth Marines who were killed in action. This ceremony was to be held in a couple of weeks on Memorial Day at the Marine Corps Cemetery in Quantico, Virginia. Fred said that he would be there and invited me to attend.

So, on a cloudy Saturday morning at the end of May, Michelle and I drove down to Quantico. We drove up the long driveway and parked the car on the grass alongside the road. There were more people than I had anticipated. How would I ever find in this crowd someone who knew my father? The folding chairs were all taken so Michelle and I sat on the grass. We picked a spot where we could see the Marine color guard and band in their dress-blue uniforms. Off to the right, on a knoll, stood three more Marines with rifles.

After the customary Memorial Day speeches and prayers, the Marines on the knoll fired three rounds from their rifles to salute those who had died. As a lone bugler played the slow sad notes of "Taps," my mind flashed back to a hillside cemetery in the Catskill Mountains of upstate New York. The year was 1948 and I was four years old. My father's body had returned from an island in the Pacific to be buried in his hometown. Family and friends gathered around his coffin to say a final good-bye. The sounds of the bugle and the guns, the flag covering my father's coffin folded neatly into a triangle and presented to my mother—they were all there again in my mind and heart, as clear and real as yesterday. I wondered to myself, "Maybe this is why I needed to come here, to continue the healing of that four-year-old boy."

When the sound of the bugle ceased, the assembly processed quietly to a clearing in the woods for the dedication ceremony. The memorial honoring the Fourth Marine Division of World War II consisted of a square marble column surrounded by a semicircle of four marble pillows. On the face of the central column was a red diamond-shaped square containing a gold number "4." This was the logo of the Fourth Marine Division. On the four marble pillows were the names and maps of the four Pacific islands on which the Fourth Marine Division had fought: Roi-Namur, Saipan, Tinian, and Iwo Jima.[1]

After the crowd dispersed, I walked slowly around the memorial. I paused before the map of Saipan and reached out to touch the stone. A new door was about to open in my search for my father. Only later did I recognize the mandala symbolism in the shape of the memorial. Even the logo of the Fourth Marines was designed like a mandala: a square diamond with a "4" in the center surrounded by the names of four islands.

MANDALA LOGO OF THE "FIGHTING FOURTH"

This mandala-like logo of the Fourth Marines would be present in every significant encounter of the succeeding months. "The Fighting Fourth," as the men of the Fourth Marines proudly referred to their division, would provide the symbolic context within which I would continue the journey to find my father and heal my soul.

When the ceremony was over, we found Fred Everett and introduced ourselves. Fred invited us to a reception where he thought I might be able to find someone who served in my father's company. The luncheon was pleasant, but once we were seated, it was difficult to move around and meet people. Since no one at our table knew my father, I felt somewhat disappointed.

As we rose to leave, Fred introduced me to someone at a neighboring table. When I repeated my name for the gentleman, another man standing behind him with his back toward me turned around and stared at me. "Are you Lt. Anthony Moore's son?" he asked. I think my heart stopped for a moment. I couldn't quite believe what was happening. No one outside my family had ever recognized me as my father's son. Struggling to control myself, I nodded. "I knew your dad," the man said. "He had reddish hair and a freckled face." The way he described my father was exactly the way my mother had always talked about him. Hearing this total stranger use the same words to describe my father felt like a visitation from another realm. The two of us looked intently at each other, both trying to contain our emotions, awestruck at the significance of our meeting.

Carl Dearborn had served briefly in my father's company, but he remembered him vividly and warmly. He also knew all the other men in the company who would have known my father and were still alive. He said he would send me their names. I could remember the name of only one man who served with my father, another officer, Chuck Landmesser. Carl said he also knew Landmesser and promised to send me his address. We talked for a while longer, but I think the emotions were too intense for both of us. It was difficult finding words to express what we were feeling, so it was easier to simply agree to keep in touch.

Carl was the only person in that crowded room who knew my father and he had found me by overhearing my name. I could not help feeling that someone must have wanted the two of us to meet.

Two days later, I received a letter from Carl Dearborn. With the letter, he enclosed a book of poems he had written in memory of the Marines who died in battle. One poem in particular caught my attention because it so aptly described my own experience.

In Memorial

The assault begins, and men go down:
they draw their final breath and widows
weep as warriors sleep,
the endless sleep of death.

A child is crying in its crib,
it feels no hurt or pain.
While far away its father falls,
he will not rise again.[2]

Reading Carl's poem, I realized why I was trying to get back to that moment when my father fell. It was the moment when, as a two-month-old infant, I received my own wound. Although I felt "no hurt or pain" at the time, healing that wound would shape the rest of my life.

I called Carl to thank him for the poems and to tell him how profoundly they had touched me. He suggested I call Gunny Hart, the Gunnery Sergeant in my father's company. After our meeting in Quantico, Carl had called Gunny to confirm his recollection that Gunny had been with my father when he was killed. Carl simply said, "Gunny is the one you want to talk to." His words felt like another message guiding my journey.

A few days later, I called Gunny Hart. He began telling me the story I had waited so long to hear. He said my father's mortar platoon was usually positioned near the company staff to the rear of the infantry platoons. Since Gunny was a member of the company staff, he and my father were usually close to each other in combat. In their first battle on Roi-Namur, Gunny and my father had even shared a foxhole.

Then Gunny described the first night on Saipan. He was no more than ten feet away from my father. They were pinned down on the beach about a hundred yards from shore. The coral on the beach was so hard they could not dig in. This left them exposed and particularly vulnerable to an artillery attack. Heavy Japanese artillery located in the hills bombarded the beach throughout the night. Not until morning did they realize that there was a Japanese spotter hidden in a smokestack just to the left of their company, targeting the artillery guns on the Marines' positions. A shell from one of those guns killed my father. Gunny was so close to my father when it happened that shrapnel from the same shell tore the pack off Gunny's back. "Your father never knew what hit him," he said. "He didn't suffer at all." Then he continued, "You can be proud of your father. He was a good Marine. Nobody can say anything against him."

Now I had some specific answers to the questions that had troubled me. The scene was different than I had imagined. When I was a child, my mother would sometimes share what she had learned about the details surrounding my father's death. She talked about the Japanese being entrenched in pillboxes and the Marines blinded by the setting sun in their eyes. She had heard that my father was wounded and died only later. When I tried to imagine the scene, I saw him lying on the beach dying as the sun was setting. Gunny Hart had given me a different set of facts—it was night and the sky was filled with artillery fire. One of those explosions killed my father instantly.

I was starting to get the true story and I hoped to learn more, but this first conversation yielded more than just a set of facts. When I mentioned I worked at Georgetown University, Gunny told me his baptismal name was Laurence ("Gunny" was a nickname for his Marine Corps rank). He was named after his uncle, Brother Laurence J. Hart, a Jesuit who worked for many years at Georgetown. Brother Hart was buried in the Jesuit cemetery on the Georgetown campus. I told Gunny that the Jesuit cemetery was right next to my office.

As I hung up the phone, I marveled at the unusual set of coincidences: my father, Anthony Moore, died next to a fellow Marine named Laurence Hart whose uncle, Laurence Hart, a Jesuit, worked and died at Georgetown where I, Anthony Moore, worked as a Jesuit. I was intrigued by the mysterious symmetry and synchronicity of the relationships among the four of us. When I tried to sketch the synchronous pattern of our relationships, I realized once again that I was working with a mandala.

MANDALA PATTERN OF SYNCHRONOUS RELATIONSHIPS

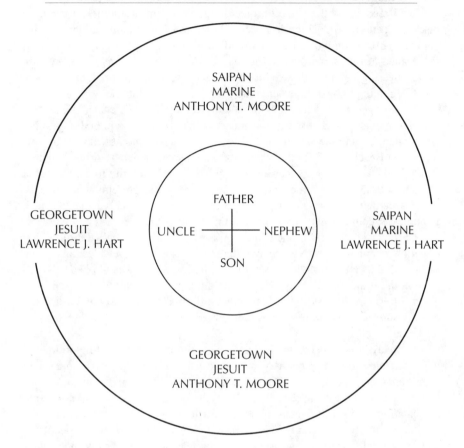

SAIPAN
MARINE
ANTHONY T. MOORE

FATHER

GEORGETOWN
JESUIT
LAWRENCE J. HART

UNCLE ——+—— NEPHEW

SAIPAN
MARINE
LAWRENCE J. HART

SON

GEORGETOWN
JESUIT
ANTHONY T. MOORE

In *Field of Dreams,* Ray Kinsella says to Terrence Mann, "You once wrote, 'There comes a time when all the cosmic tumblers have clicked into place, and the universe opens itself up for a few seconds, to show you what is possible.'" When I discovered the mandala pattern in our relationships, it was as though the cosmic tumblers clicked into place to show me how closely my father's story and mine were interconnected. The threads that knit our lives together were much more intertwined than I could have imagined. When my father died next to Laurence Hart on Saipan, his uncle and namesake, Brother Laurence Hart, was working as a Jesuit at Georgetown University. Thirty-six years later, I would begin working as a Jesuit on the same campus where Brother Laurence Hart lived and now lies buried. Every day for ten years I walked by the burial site of a Jesuit brother whose nephew was with my father when he died.

My life seemed to be connected to my father's death in a way I never antic-

ipated. Although I resisted drawing any hasty conclusions from these coincidences, I recognized the value of attending to such synchronicities in trying to
discern a pattern of meaning in my life. Learning about Laurence Hart and his
uncle reconfirmed my belief that I would do well to honor these synchronicities
if I wanted to find some meaning in the random violence of my father's death.
By discovering a pattern of meaning in the details surrounding my father's death,
I was beginning to heal the wound that his death inflicted in me.

Encouraged by my conversation with Gunny Hart, I decided to contact
Chuck Landmesser. Chuck was someone who had been close to both my father
and mother. During the war, he and his wife had shared a home with my parents
in Laguna Beach, California. My parents were also godparents for his daughter.
When I was young, my mother and Chuck's wife would write to each other at
Christmas time. I even remember exchanging Christmas presents with his chil-
dren. Although our families had lost contact over the years, I knew Chuck
Landmesser could provide an important link to my father.

Carl Dearborn had sent me Chuck's California address. I called information
to get his phone number. Nervously, I dialed the phone. When Chuck answered,
I told him, "I'm Tony Moore's son." When he responded, I could hear his surprise in the sound of his voice. He said he did not even recall my father having
a son. I told him I would be in Southern California in early July and asked if I
could visit him. He said he would be delighted and would send me directions to
his home.

I already knew this trip to California was an important part of my journey. I
was scheduled to give a one-day workshop using *Field of Dreams* to explain
Jung's approach to inner work. The workshop was part of the national conference
of the Association for Psychological Type, the group to whom I gave my first
presentation on *Field of Dreams* two years earlier in Richmond, Virginia. During
the intervening two years, my involvement with my father's story had deepened
and intensified. I was looking forward to sharing the results of my inner work
with others. But I was especially excited about this trip because the conference
was to be held in Newport Beach, just ten miles up the coast from Laguna Beach.

Often in the past I joked that I was born in Cohoes, N.Y., but conceived in
Laguna Beach, California. Anyone familiar with these two locations would
appreciate why I was more enthusiastic about the place of my conception than
the place of my birth—a Southern California seaside resort versus an aging
northeastern mill town. More importantly, Laguna was the place where my parents spent most of their one year together as a married couple. My mother always
described the time and the place with affection and longing. She said my father
often talked about returning to live in Laguna after the war. When he died, my
mother chose to live with her parents in Cohoes. We never went back to Laguna,
although we often talked about it. This trip to Southern California felt like a journey back to my roots, back to the place where my parents shared their one year
of happiness and where they said their last good-bye.

As I stood in a hotel conference room in Newport Beach and talked of Ray Kinsella and his father, I looked out the window facing south toward Laguna and thought of my own journey to find my father. The day after my workshop, I rented a car and drove down the Coast Highway to Laguna Beach. I was trying to find the house where my parents lived, but I had only a vague description of its location and no address. I looked for buildings that appeared old enough to have been there in the 1940s. I imagined my parents walking down the quaint, sunny streets holding hands. Although I was unable to find the house, I enjoyed spending the day soaking up the local atmosphere of the art community that now inhabits Laguna. Driving up into the hills and looking out over the Pacific, I understood where I got my love of the beach. Surrounded by the beautiful homes and scenery of the Laguna hills, I could not help lamenting what might have been—if only my father had survived.

The next day, I drove east toward the desert to visit Chuck Landmesser. He lived in Twentynine Palms, a desert community located on the edge of the Mohave between the Marine Corps Training Center and Joshua Tree National Park. Driving along deep in thought and filled with anticipation, I had the feeling that I would somehow meet my father on this journey, but I did not know how. As I approached Chuck's wood-frame house, I noticed the American flag and, right below it, the red and gold Marine Corps flag flying in the breeze on a high pole in the front yard. I read in this simple gesture Chuck's way of symbolizing and honoring the purpose of our meeting.

As I got out of the car to greet him, I felt a little like Ray Kinsella, not knowing what to say to his father when he first appears on the field. Chuck is a very fit and ruddy eighty-year-old. He invited me in and showed me around the house that he had built with his own hands, section by section, over the previous twenty years. His wife, Vivian, prepared a lunch of baby-back ribs and beans.

After lunch, we sat and talked in a room filled with Marine Corps and World War II memorabilia: photographs, flags, weapons, etc. I wondered how my father would have felt visiting his old Marine Corps buddy after all these years. I could sense my father's presence on the fringe of our conversation, but I did not know how to invite him more directly into its center. Although I longed deeply for some word from Chuck that would make my father come alive for me, I was reluctant to force the issue. I was trying to be patient and allow my father to reveal his presence gradually and in his own way. I understood that visiting Chuck Landmesser was a symbolic action that required attentive waiting.

Together, we looked slowly through several albums of photographs from the war years with Chuck providing a commentary on the people and events. Then, Chuck suggested we take a ride out to Joshua Tree National Park. Together we climbed into his weathered blue pick-up and headed south into the park. Joshua Tree is nearly half a million acres of wilderness where the high Mohave Desert meets the lower Colorado Desert. Its stark beauty calms the spirit and touches the soul. As we rode along, I gradually became aware of the layers of meaning in this trip into the wilderness. Chuck explained that the Joshua tree was named after the Israelite leader who led the people in battle while Moses prayed to God with his arms lifted up to heaven. When early settlers saw the large branches of the Joshua tree reaching outward and upward into the clear blue desert sky, they were reminded of the outstretched arms of Moses as he prayed in the wilderness.

Entering the park, we drove eastward into the lower Colorado Desert. The road led continually downward through arid land covered with creosote bush and small stands of spidery ocotillo and jumping cholla cactus. Down, down, down we went for twenty-five miles over dusty desert roads in 100+ degree temperatures. At the end of our long, hot descent, we arrived at an oasis surrounded by fifty-foot palm trees. In the shade of the trees, water bubbled to the surface from an underground stream while bees buzzed in the mud created by the water as it spread out in numerous rivulets. About thirty feet from the spring was a circular stone approximately five feet in diameter. Chuck explained that the stone was used by prospectors for extracting gold from the muddy soil washed up by the underground spring.

When I saw the circular stone, I suddenly became aware of all the Jungian symbolism in our journey. The journey out into the wilderness and the steady descent to the bubbling oasis represented an interior descent to the deeper layers of the unconscious from which psychic energy bubbles up. The image of prospectors extracting gold from the muddy soil recalled the labors of medieval alchemists trying to transform gross matter into gold. For Jung, the alchemists' labors symbolized the interior process of individuation in which the gross matter of the unconscious was transmuted into the psychic gold of the self. The circular stone used by the prospectors to extract the gold was actually in the shape of a mandala, a symbol for the wholeness of the self—the goal of the individuation process.

For those who had eyes to see, there was more at work in this journey than just a sun-drenched ride through the desert. By letting the symbols speak to me, I came to see this trip as a journey of transformation moving me toward a deeper sense of wholeness. The symbols helped me to trust that the wound of my father's absence was somehow being healed through this journey into the desert. The gross matter of my psychic wound was being transmuted into gold through the marvelous alchemy of spiritual journey. The gold was the integrity of my own soul.

When we finished exploring the oasis, Chuck took a photograph of me standing by the stream in front of the huge palm trees. Then we got back in the truck and began an ascent up through the Colorado Desert across the transition zone into the higher, cooler and wetter Mohave Desert, a landscape dominated by Joshua trees and large outcroppings of red rock. From the Mohave Desert, we climbed higher and higher into the Little San Bernardino Mountains.

As we wound our way up the mountains, I tried to draw Chuck into conversation about my father. I was waiting for him to tell me something about my father that would make him more real for me. Initially, Chuck seemed to find it easier to talk about stories that did not refer directly to my father. At times, it seemed as though Chuck was talking more to my father than to me. It was as if two war buddies who had not seen each other for fifty years were simply getting caught up on the intervening years.

Eventually, Chuck began to describe their time aboard ship as they headed toward their first battle on Roi-Namur. I asked if my father ever said anything that would indicate he had some premonition of what would happen to him. Chuck's immediate answer was, "No, no one ever thought something would happen to them. They always figured it would be the other guy. If you really stopped to think it could happen to you, you wouldn't be able to do it."

Then, perhaps sensing that I was looking for something specific to hold on to, he said:

> There is something I will always remember about your dad, and that is the way he felt about your mother, Palma. Other guys might talk about their wives in a way that was not very respectful, but 'A.T.' would never do that. There was only one love for your father and that was your mother.

His words touched me so deeply that at first I almost interrupted him so he would not say any more. I felt like I was getting more than I had anticipated. All I was able to say was, "My mother returned his love; she never remarried." Chuck nodded his head and said, "I know."

Maybe this was the gift I had come to receive. In Chuck's words, I could hear my father speaking to me, telling me how much he loved my mother and by implication how much he loved me, the fruit of their love. I then found myself answering for my mother and me, telling my father that we had never forgotten him, that no one had ever taken his place in her heart or mine. When I heard Chuck answer, "I know," I heard my father reassuring us that our love had reached him and that he had been with us all these years. This was the message he wanted to leave with me: that my parents' love for each other and for me was the one truth to remember and live by, that I should live my life in the same way, letting all else in my life be shaped by my love for Michelle and the boys. These consoling thoughts came to me as I gazed out the truck window at a golden desert panorama receding below me.

When we reached the top of the mountain, we left the truck and climbed a short distance to Key's View. Before our feet, the mountain dropped straight down to the desert valley below. Standing on an overlook 5000 feet above sea level, we could see nearly seventy miles out across the valley and mountains below. As I stood on this mountain peak, a feeling of awe came over me. I was well aware of the archetypal symbolism of mountaintops. Moses' encounter with God on Mount Sinai was not far from my thoughts. Then, I thought of how my father had spoken to me through this man standing beside me. Recalling how the wise old man archetype can stand in for the father, I realized that Chuck Landmesser was for me a personal incarnation of the wise old man.

Standing on the mountaintop with my wisdom figure and guide helped me recognize the deeper archetypal symbolism of our journey together. In travelling over the physical landscape, Chuck and I had descended into the desert wilderness, then ascended to the view from the mountain peak. It was amazing how closely our journey conformed to the archetypal pattern of descent and ascent. I was reminded again of Dante and Virgil descending into the underworld, then ascending the mountain of Purgatory. I had discovered the same pattern in *Field of Dreams* when Ray Kinsella descended the winding ramps of Fenway Park with Terrence Mann and later walked with Doc Graham across the top of a stairway leading from one street level to the next. Now I was following the same pattern of descent and ascent, symbolizing my journey to wholeness. By talking to Chuck about my father's death, I descended into the underworld of my own unconscious psychic pain. Then, I ascended upward to receive the healing insight of my father's lasting love, a love that is present especially in my love for my wife and sons.

The archetypal pattern of the journey told me my personal story was part of a bigger story, a story rooted deeply within the human psyche and repeated down through the ages. It was the story of a journey down through the darker, hidden recesses of the soul and a gradual ascent to a healing vision of the meaning in one's life. I was so caught up by the experience that I wished I could celebrate a Eucharist there on the mountaintop with this man who brought my father to me. Hesitant to voice such thoughts with someone I had met only hours before, I simply offered a silent prayer of thanksgiving and commented to Chuck that it seemed like a great place to have a Mass. He concurred and mentioned that an Easter sunrise service was usually held on the spot.

Later, I found a description of an incident in Jung's life that bore an uncanny resemblance to my experience at Key's View. When Jung was 14, his father took him on a trip to a mountain village. Standing at the foot of an enormous mountain towering over the village, Jung's father pressed a ticket into the boy's hand and told him he could ride to the peak of the mountain alone. Jung described the experience in the following way:

> With a tremendous puffing, the wonderful locomotive shook and rattled me up to the dizzy heights where ever-new abysses and panoramas opened out before my gaze, until at last I stood on the peak in the strange thin air, looking into unimaginable distances. "Yes," I thought, "this is it, my world, the real world, the secret,...where one can be without having to ask anything." It was all very solemn, and I felt one had to be polite and silent up here, for one was in God's world. Here it was physically present. This was the best and most precious gift my father had ever given me.[3]

In addition to the similar setting and tone of our experiences, what struck me about Jung's account was that he described his experience of God's closeness as a gift from his father. Reading Jung's account caused me to reflect on how much my own experience of God had been a precious gift from my father. I could not imagine what my experience of God would have been if I had not been compelled to deal with my father's death. Realizing the crucial role my father's death has played in my spiritual journey helped me understand how a deep psychic wound may contain a hidden gift, a gift that can be discovered by following a pathway of healing.

In my conversation and trip with Chuck Landmesser, my journey to connect to my father reached a milestone. Where the road led from there was still unclear, but something had been achieved, a corner had been turned. Through symbolic action, I was learning how to listen to my father's voice. I now knew I could trust the pathway forward wherever it might lead.

The next stage of my journey began at the annual reunion of the Fourth Marine Division held in San Antonio, Texas. I planned my itinerary so I would arrive in time for a memorial service scheduled for 6:00 p.m. on a Friday night. The ceremony was to be held on the square in front of the Alamo. About an hour before the service was scheduled to begin, I walked over to the old Spanish mission, hoping to get a deeper sense of the place. I was conscious of the significance of place for doing symbolic work. Since I knew this would be an important occasion, I wanted to properly honor the space beforehand.

The last time I had been in San Antonio I was a college sophomore returning home from a summer in Mexico. Nevertheless, the image of the Alamo was still vivid in my memory. As I approached the structure, it felt like a familiar place. I walked slowly through the large wooden doors and entered the former church, now a museum. Although the space was no longer used for religious services, a sacred aura permeated the environment. I strolled reflectively around the mission, conscious of the lives that were sacrificed on that battlefield. It felt as though the blood of the soldiers who died there had consecrated the ground.

By the time I finished my meditative tour of the Alamo, Marine veterans and their wives were starting to gather in the plaza in front of the mission. I walked toward the last row of folding chairs so I would have a better view of the whole event. The sun was setting behind us, casting a golden red glow on the front of the Alamo. A Marine Corps color guard marched up the aisle to the front of the assembly. As they passed by me, I was surprised to see how young they appeared. Then I thought of how young my father and these old veterans were when they went off to war.

The ceremony began. We pledged allegiance to the flag, said a prayer for the deceased of each religious denomination, and sang *God Bless America*. Then, a tall, retired Marine colonel with a white crew cut walked slowly to the podium, leaning heavily on his cane. In a strong and moving voice, he read a poem called *The Empty Chair*. The poem was addressed to soldiers who died in battle. An empty chair was placed on the dais in memory of the fallen Marines. As I listened to the poem and stared at the empty chair, I could see my father sitting there. I sensed that many others around me were having similar visions.

I went to San Antonio looking for my father. There I witnessed the esteem and affection in which those who survived held him and his brother heroes. I was touched to see so much emotion expressed by those tough old Marines as they remembered friends who had died. The presence of those fallen Marines in the hearts and minds of their buddies, fifty years after the war, made my father somehow more real, more substantial, less a ghostly figure flitting across my consciousness. His presence in that assembly was as real as the empty chair on the stage. It was made real by the palpable honor and fidelity with which those aging men around me remembered his sacrifice. The words and ritual of *The Empty Chair* became a sacrament of his presence.

As the old colonel finished the poem, three World War II biplanes flew over us, scattering sands from the four Pacific Islands where members of the Fourth Marine Division had fought and died. The grounds of the Alamo hallowed by the blood of fallen warriors were now reconsecrated with the sands of other distant battlefields. The service concluded with the playing of "Taps" and everyone singing the *Marine Corps Hymn*.

The ceremony and ritual of the memorial service moved and comforted my soul. Something deep inside was being stirred and healed. As I walked along with the dispersing crowds, I thought, "This is where I am supposed to be. This is what I am meant to do."

Later that night, after supper, I walked alone down along the riverwalk that follows the San Antonio River as it winds its way below the streets of the city. I was stimulated by the vitality of this subterranean world of restaurants, shops, and people flowing just below the surface of the city. It symbolized for me the vital energy of the unconscious flowing below the level of consciousness.

As I turned a corner into a pleasant grove of trees and shrubs, I was suddenly surprised by a lifesize statue of St. Anthony. At first, I wondered why there would be a religious symbol in a city park. Up to that moment, the significance of the city's name had completely escaped my notice. Then, as I stared at the statue of San Antonio's patron saint, I recalled a small statue of St. Anthony that stood on my mother's dresser. I had given the statue to my mother as a Christmas gift more than thirty years earlier. My mother had a special devotion to St. Anthony because my father was born on the saint's feast day and was named after him. I chose the statue as a gift in recognition of my mother's devotion to the saint and the saint's relationship to my father.

Now, an incredibly lifelike St. Anthony stood before me. His face seemed oddly younger than I would have expected. I reflected that he appeared to be the same age my father was when he died. He held a small boy in his arms. As I looked at the boy I wondered how it would have felt to be held by my father. Cherishing the image and the feelings it evoked, I let the symbol speak to me. I could almost feel my father's protective arms wrapped around me. Then, I offered a quiet prayer of gratitude for the experience and continued along the path, more convinced than ever of my father's companionship on this journey. I was beginning to feel as though he was trying to find me as much as I was trying to find him.

The following morning, as I waited to be seated for breakfast in the hotel restaurant, I found myself standing in line next to the stately gentleman whose reading of *The Empty Chair* had touched me so deeply the previous evening. Somewhat embarrassed, I told him how much his reading had meant to me. As he thanked me, the waitress approached and directed me to my table. I wanted to talk to him further, but I felt a little awkward. When I noticed that he was also dining alone, I decided to overcome my shyness. I walked over to his table and asked him whether he would like some company for breakfast or prefer to eat alone. Graciously, he said he would be delighted to have the company.

When I sat down and introduced myself, he said, "You look awfully young to be with all these World War II vets." I replied, "I'm here because my father was a Marine who was killed the first night on Saipan." He then asked what unit my father was in. When I told him, "3-I-24" (24th Marine Regiment, 3rd Battalion, I Company), he looked quickly at the nametag pinned on my jacket; a flash of recognition and surprise swept across his face. "Is your mother Palma?" he asked. I was stunned. Here, across the table from me, sat a stranger who knew my father so well that after fifty years he could still remember my mother's name.

His name was Walter Ridlon. He and his wife, Signe, had been close friends of my parents during the war. He recalled how they used to gather around the piano for an evening of singing and dancing at my parents' home in Laguna. Then, as though it was only yesterday, he recalled an incident I never heard my mother mention. "This may sound funny," he said, "but I remember coming home one night and my wife saying to me, 'Why did you take all of Tony's money?'" Not knowing what she was talking about, Walt asked what she meant. Then she explained how my mother had visited and told her that my father had lost all his money to Walt in a dice game. Walt told his wife that he had not realized it was all the money my parents had to get them through the month. He offered to return the money to my father and let him pay it back gradually. His wife answered, "Don't bother. I already gave all the money back to Palma and you're never getting any of it."

The two of us broke into laughter. We were no longer strangers. My father had brought us together. I could see in Walt's face how much he enjoyed telling this story. It simply burst forth as though it had been inside him all these years just waiting to be told. As I listened to the story, I could feel my father coming to life. His human shortcomings made him more alive, more real for me. He was no longer a perfect, idealized hero, but a man of flesh and blood who could be foolish, make mistakes and get into the kind of trouble from which his wife had to rescue him.

Learning about my father's peccadilloes was a liberating experience. Trying to be the perfect son of an ideal father was a burden that often got in the way of my being myself. I wondered whether I inherited my incompetence as a gambler from my father. Then I thought about some of my other shortcomings and wondered whether they might also be a gift from him, and therefore something to be prized. Just thinking about my father in this way created a more balanced hero archetype for me to follow. Another gap in my fatherless childhood was being filled.

Walt proceeded to describe how he had been no more than thirty yards from my father that first night on Saipan. Because of the confusion on the battlefield, he learned about my father's death only several days later. When the battle for Saipan was finally over, Walt went to the battlefield cemetery looking for the graves of his friends. On my father's grave marker he noticed there was only a name with no rank indicated. Troubled by the unusual omission, Walt inquired about my father's grave with the graves records officer. He was told that when my father's body was found, the dog tags were missing. Without any dog tags, the grave crew identified my father's body by the name they found on a field message book in his pocket. Walt was concerned about the accuracy of the identification so he asked to be shown where they had found the body. When they showed him the location, it confirmed for him that it was indeed my father's body because he remembered the position of my father's unit during the first night of fighting.

Although Walt had reassured me about the identification of my father's body, I could not help wondering what had happened to cause my father to lose his dog tags. The difficulty in identifying his body might also explain why my family had not received official confirmation of my father's death until two months after his death. In trying to get as close as possible to the details of my father's death, I now had some new facts to work with, but my conversation with Walt Ridlon also raised a troubling question: what exactly was the nature of the injury that killed my father? Gunny Hart had said my father never suffered, he never knew what hit him. Almost not wanting to think the thought but unable to avoid it, I now concluded that whatever happened that night separated my father from the dog tags hanging around his neck. Was it some kind of a head wound? How much damage was there that made it so difficult to identify him? The questions came unsolicited, but they came nonetheless. Although I was not ready to pursue them further, I knew that eventually I would have to.

When we finished breakfast, Walt said his wife would love to meet me. Later that afternoon, I sat with Walt and Signe in their hotel room as they recounted the good times they had shared with my parents and the other Marine couples who rented homes in Laguna Beach. Being with them was like being invited into the circle of friends with whom my parents enjoyed the one year they had together.

Signe wanted to know all about my mother. Because of my mother's failing memory, I knew she would not have been able to join in the reminiscing. Nevertheless, I felt that she and my father were with us. They were present in a playful, fun-loving way, a way in which I had never before pictured them. In my imagination, I saw five young couples gathered around a piano singing and laughing. My father had his arm around my mother and she smiled at him as he sang loudly but slightly off-key. It was 1944 and we were all together again.

From the expressions on their faces, I could see that our being together was bringing back similar images for Walt and Signe. Signe mentioned how much I reminded her of my father. I think we all felt a presence that we could not define but we knew was real. I had the odd feeling that my father was using me to connect to people who were close to him. It was as though I stood between heaven and earth, between time and eternity, and love passed through me from one realm to the other. It was a feeling that would often return as I talked with people who knew my father.

That evening we all went to the closing dinner of the reunion. I was looking forward to meeting Charlie Eaton, the only member of my father's platoon attending the reunion. I had already spoken on the phone with his wife, Helen, who told me how much he was looking forward to our meeting. Although Charlie's speech was impaired by a stroke he suffered several years earlier, I could see the excitement in his eyes when I approached his table and introduced myself. He was so thrilled to meet me that his body shook all over as he laughed and struggled to communicate.

With Helen's help, Charlie told me his daughter was born in February of 1944. My parents were also expecting at the time. To tease Charlie, my father kept boasting that his baby would be a boy. He said my father was elated when he finally received news of my birth. I knew from my mother that my father was happy about my birth, but it was a special gift to hear about his joyful reaction from a fellow Marine who was with him when he got the news. I was also glad to know that my father was the kind of officer who could joke with his men.

Charlie said he was lying on the beach next to my father when he was killed. Charlie was severely wounded by the same explosion that took my father's life.

Then, he showed me a photograph of my father standing in a field with several other Marines. My father's face was barely visible because his helmet was tilted down over his eyes. On the back of the photograph, Charlie had written the word, "Lieutenant." My father had been Charlie's lieutenant. He had saved the photograph over the years as a memento of their relationship. As I looked at the photograph, Charlie gave me a thumbs-up sign and said, "Your father was a real man." I nodded my head in gratitude and held him by the shoulder. He gestured that he wanted me to keep the photograph. Our eyes filled with tears as we smiled to each other, recognizing what this brief meeting meant for both of us.

Next morning, on the ride to the airport, I reflected on my experience with the statue of St. Anthony on the San Antonio riverwalk. The synchronicity of this event opened up a way of knowing that further confirmed for me my father's guiding presence on this journey. It seemed as though he was intent on making sure I got the message that I was not alone on this trip to San Antonio. I smiled and thanked him for his presence, knowing this was only one more stop on our journey together.

The next phase of my journey involved a series of events that culminated the following year at the annual reunion of the Fourth Marines in Norfolk, Virginia. Soon after our Memorial Day meeting in Quantico, Fred Everett had called to invite me to be the main speaker at the reunion. Even before he called, I had a premonition that speaking to this group would be a natural outcome of my journey. So when Fred called, I was both surprised and reassured that my premonitions were right on target. I felt as though my father wanted to say something to these men and that he was going to use me as his messenger. My only anxiety was whether I would be worthy of the task. Could I give the kind of speech those Marine veterans would find worthwhile and meaningful? Before I could get too entangled in my own performance anxieties, another synchronicity appeared, revealing once again the mysterious forces that were guiding my walk between heaven and earth.

After our Quantico meeting, Fred Everett started sending me copies of the newsletter published by the Fourth Marine Association. The newsletters carried photographs and stories about local chapter reunions and notices about the recent deaths of members. There were also photographs from the war years sent in by people attempting to contact the individuals pictured in the photographs. When these newsletters arrived, I would usually flip through them quickly looking for any reference to my father's unit, then leave them on the kitchen counter for subsequent reading.

One evening while I was upstairs writing, I heard Michelle scream from the kitchen below, "Oh, my God, I can't believe it!" The note of shock in her voice frightened me. I rushed downstairs not knowing what to expect. Michelle had been casually leafing through an issue of the newsletter when she spotted her maiden name, "Dewey." She handed me the newsletter and pointed to a picture of five Marines. "That's my Uncle Ray," she said. The caption under the photograph listed five names including "R. Dewey." Three of the names, including her uncle's, were followed by the letters "KIA," indicating the men had been killed in action. One of the two survivors had submitted the photograph to the newsletter hoping to make contact with the only other survivor in the group.

Michelle knew that her uncle was a Marine and that he was killed on Iwo Jima, but until that moment we had no idea he and my father served in the same division. Later, we learned that Ray fought in all four battles (Roi-Namur, Saipan, Tinian, and Iwo Jima) and died in the last week of the Fourth Marines' final battle on Iwo Jima in 1945.

Michelle's Uncle Ray was the youngest of eleven children in a closely-knit Irish Catholic family. Although Michelle never met her uncle, she grew up hearing stories about this wonderful young man revered by his family as a hero.

Looking at Ray's picture, both of us could see the strong family resemblance between Michelle's uncle and her father.

The synchronicities between my father and Michelle's uncle were hard to ignore: two young men, the youngest of their large Irish Catholic families, serving in the same Marine division and fighting on the same beaches of Roi-Namur and Saipan. They probably never met each other, but now they were related in a strange, almost mystical way through two people who, fifty years later, remembered them both with warm affection and a deep sense of personal loss.

Up to this point, Michelle had encouraged my efforts to learn more about my father, but she had remained personally uninvolved in my quest—the synchronicity of her uncle fighting and dying as a member of the same Marine division changed all that. Like Annie Kinsella who helped her husband pack for his trip to Boston because of her synchronous dream, Michelle became a part of my pilgrimage when we realized the synchronous connection between my father and her father's kid brother. It was now clear to both of us that this was not simply my story but our story. It was not only about my father and me but also about Michelle and me. Whatever mysterious forces were drawing me forward on this journey of discovery were also at work in my relationship with Michelle. Ray Kinsella's comment to his wife sounded like words of advice aimed at us: "When primal forces of nature tell you to do something," Ray had argued, "the prudent thing is not to quibble over details."

When Michelle and I first met, we often kidded that destiny brought us together. Half jokingly, we would say our fathers in heaven had arranged for us to find each other. Now, the connection between my father and Michelle's uncle appeared to confirm our belief. Clearly, our lives were intertwined even before we were born, and in a way we had never expected. When I told Fred Everett that Michelle's uncle was also a member of the Fighting Fourth, he wrote a story about us for the newsletter and invited Michelle to join me in speaking at the Fourth Marines reunion in Norfolk.

The reunion was scheduled for the weekend of June 10-12, 1994. A few months before the reunion I received a letter from Al Arsenault, the captain of my father's company. The letter was addressed to the men and honorary members of 3-I-24. Arsenault was trying to gather as many as possible for the reunion because it was also the 80th birthday of Gunny Hart. I was thrilled that a special effort was being made to reassemble the members of my father's old company for this occasion. It would increase my chances of finding some men who knew my father well enough to remember a small detail or anecdote about him, anything that might make him come alive for me.

I was also struck by the fact that the reason for this special effort was to honor a man who had been near my father when he died. Gunny and I had already spoken on the phone, but the reunion would offer me an opportunity to question him in greater depth. When Walt Ridlon told me about my father's missing dog tags, my first thought was to ask Gunny Hart what he could add by way of explanation. Since I did not feel comfortable having this conversation on the phone, I was glad I would have a chance to speak with Gunny in person.

At the annual reunions of the Fourth Marines, a large ballroom is set up with 70-80 large round tables spread throughout the room. These circular tables serve as gathering points for the various units that made up the division. If you are trying to find someone, the best place to start is at the table assigned to that person's unit. I was familiar with the routine because of my trip to San Antonio the previous year. So, the first evening we arrived, I could not wait to bring Michelle to the ballroom to find out who was there from my father's company. When we found the table for 3-I-24, I was overwhelmed to find so many people already there. There were probably twenty-five Marines plus some wives. I worried whether it would be possible to have an intimate conversation with anyone in such a large gathering.

When I approached the table, a couple of men recognized me from the year before. They started to introduce me to the others at the table. Some of the men had joined the unit after my father was killed, so they were polite but did not have much to say. But the seven men who remembered my father formed a circle around me and were eager to talk. One man told me my father was relatively quiet. Unlike some of the other officers, my father never yelled or raised his voice, but when he gave an order, he expected his men to obey. As the man spoke, others nodded in assent, echoing the opinion that my father was soft-spoken but clear about his responsibility as an officer.

As I listened to the men talking warmly about my father's qualities and characteristics, I could feel the respect and affection they still had for him. One man in particular stood out for me. His name was Burke Dixon. He was from Georgia and he was a squad leader in my father's platoon. Burke stood about five feet, five inches. His round ruddy face and southern accent reinforced the warmth and sincerity that emanated so clearly from somewhere deep inside. I was immediately drawn to him because of the manner in which he talked about my father. A sense of intimacy and respect, verging on reverence, shone through his recollections of my father.

Burke told me my father was his favorite officer. They were together from the very beginning when the company was first formed at Camp Pendleton. "Your father was a great listener," he said. "You could always go to him with your problems. We were just young kids away from home for the first time so you can imagine how many problems we had. Your father would always listen and try to help. After he was killed things were never quite the same for me. When the war was over, I told my wife if we ever had a son I wanted to name him Anthony after Lt. Moore."

Burke proceeded to recall little incidents that revealed the kind of man and officer my father was. Once on Maui, Burke was on his way off the base when he realized he had forgotten his cap. Since he did not have enough time to go back to his tent, he just stopped at my father's tent and asked him if he had an extra cap. My father said, "Here," and flipped his cap across the bunk to him. Later, in town, Burke was stopped by the Shore Patrol because he was wearing corporal stripes on his shirtsleeve and a lieutenant's bar on his cap. Burke burst into laughter as he reminisced, "Your father almost got me court-martialed for that little gesture."

On another occasion, the weapons platoons were on a practice range firing their 60mm mortars. While my father's platoon waited their turn to fire, my father walked forward and stood behind the other platoons as they fired, close enough to hear the coordinates they were using. Platoon after platoon missed the target, overshooting it or falling short, then adjusting their coordinates to zero in on the target. When it came time for my father's platoon to fire, he whispered to Burke, "Set the coordinates for 275 yards." Burke followed my father's order and scored a direct hit on the target with the first shot. Watching and listening to the other platoons as they missed the target, my father had calculated the correct coordinates and provided them to his men. That day my father's men came away from the practice range feeling confident about themselves and their lieutenant, knowing that he would take care of them in whatever way he could.

Burke then described another incident on Maui that showed how my father related to his troops. The company had been practicing maneuvers in fields of burning sugar cane to prepare for the kinds of battle conditions that might occur on the Pacific islands. Although the men did not know it at the time, their next destination was the island of Saipan where sugar cane was the primary crop. As the company was marching back to the camp along both sides of the road, someone reached in and blew the horn of an empty truck parked alongside the road. Captain Arsenault halted the company and demanded to know who had blown the horn. My father and a few of his men had observed the culprit. When Burke whispered to my father, "I'm not going to tell," my father replied, "Neither am I." As Burke recounted the story more than fifty years after the event, I could see how much it still meant to him. "Lt. Moore did not put on airs like some of the other officers. He was more like one of the guys. He was natural. You could always talk to him."

Talking with Burke Dixon was a powerful encounter with my father's spirit because I could actually feel the impact of his presence in the life of another person. Clearly, my father had a profound influence on Burke's life and the man he became. As Burke spoke, a complex set of emotions and insights began to stir within me. On one level, I was proud of my father. He was the kind of man other men respected and even loved. He was down-to-earth, a regular guy, someone who cared about his men and tried to help them. He was a role model who could have inspired me. On another level, however, I felt an unavoidable sadness that I had missed being raised by this man, that I never had the chance to go to him with my problems, to be the beneficiary of his advice and counsel, to experience firsthand his love and caring. My customary pain of never knowing my father seemed to deepen and increase as I realized what a wonderful father he would have been. He fathered those young Marines so well. Maybe he was giving them the fathering he wished he could have given me, if only he had had the chance.

On the deepest level, however, my feelings were not those of sadness or regret but of recognition. I recognized in my father the kind of man that I tried to be. So much of what comes naturally to me seemed also to have been a part of him. When I heard Burke describe my father as a good listener, someone you could always go to with your problems, I recalled how as a new teacher at Georgetown, I would sit and listen to college freshmen as they described their struggles to adjust to college and to find a direction for their lives. I also recalled how I loved to give retreats and spiritual direction because they gave me an opportunity to connect with other people on such a deep and intimate level. I now recognized how much this natural ability that had so shaped my life was a gift from my father. I could feel him living and breathing in me as I did the work I most like to do. More importantly, I could see my father in my relationship with my sons. As I recalled sitting with my eighteen-year-old son at two in the morning discussing his problems, I realized that I had become the father my father never had a chance to be.

Several months later, I discovered an ancient Indian belief that helped me understand what I experienced in talking with Burke Dixon:

> There occurs at the moment of death the transference of a father's personality into that of his son so that into the son is carried over the secret vitality of the father, so that the father may continue to live again in the son.[4]

When I read these words, something dropped into place. I recognized in my own unique personality the "secret vitality" of my father's ongoing life within me. What others loved in me and what I most enjoyed about myself were gifts of his presence. If I wanted to be with my father, I only needed to live the life I had been given and to do it with enthusiasm and gratitude.

My conversation with Burke also supplied the kind of intimate details about my father's life as a Marine lieutenant that I had been seeking. These concrete details expanded and enriched my image of my father as a war hero, thereby creating a hero archetype with which I could more readily identify. He was not only dedicated and committed but also warm and caring.

As Burke Dixon and I finished talking, Gunny Hart arrived. Gunny was an incredibly fit eighty-year-old. With almost a full head of white hair and a bronze Florida tan, he looked like a man in his 60s. Gunny was with I Company from its inception. At thirty years of age, he was the "Ol' Man" of the company. My father and the other officers were in their early 20s and most of the enlisted men were still teenagers. Because of his age, rank, and previous Marine Corps experience, Gunny became the father figure of the company. Seeing how he looked at eighty, I could well imagine the impact he must have had on these men when he was in his prime.

Gunny walked with a slight limp because his right leg was shattered on Iwo Jima. Although he bicycled every day to keep in shape, standing for long periods caused the wound to flare up. He asked if we could sit while we talked. Both of us had difficulty hearing over the noise of the surrounding conversations so we pulled a couple of chairs aside and leaned in toward each other.

Gunny began by retelling how he had shared a foxhole with my father on Roi-Namur and how they were also positioned near each other the first night on Saipan. He mentioned the heavy artillery bombardment that hit them on Saipan and how exposed they were: "We were trying to dig into the beach but the coral was so hard my hands were bleeding from the digging." Then I told him what I had learned from Walt Ridlon, that the graves crew had difficulty identifying my father's body because he was missing his dog tags. I didn't have to say anymore. I think he knew what I was looking for and I think he wanted to tell me. Without much emotion but quietly and sincerely, he said, "Your father took a direct hit from mortar or artillery. He was blown apart. I was so close that some of his body parts may have hit me. Many other men were killed or wounded at the same time."

These were the facts that I had both sought and feared. When I finally heard them, all I felt was a vague numbness. That handsome young face that stared back at me from countless photographs had been destroyed beyond all recognition.

Although Gunny had answered my most troubling question, I still wanted to know more. I wanted to be as present to the event as possible, but I did not want to press Gunny to reveal more than he felt comfortable doing. Perhaps sensing my dilemma, Gunny proceeded to describe his own experience of being wounded. "I knew I would be hit sometime," he said. "I carried a St. Christopher medal that I used to rub, praying that when I got hit it would be in the legs and in daylight." He went on to explain that one had a better chance of surviving a leg wound and the wounded could only be evacuated in daylight. During the night, Marines would never move because the standing orders were, "If it moves, shoot it." Only the Japanese moved at night. When Gunny was hit in the legs on Iwo Jima, it was 7:30 in the morning.

The prayers of one young Marine had been answered and here he was fifty years later sharing the story with me. I wondered what my father's prayers were that night on Saipan and whether they were answered.

When Gunny and I finished talking, I felt I needed time to take in everything I had heard that evening. I could not absorb any more information, so Michelle and I excused ourselves and said we would see everyone at the banquet next evening.

I spent the next day going over my speech. Unlike most other things I have written, this speech seemed to write itself. While I was writing it, I kept before me on my desk a photograph of my father standing in front of his tent on Maui.

I asked him to guide me so I could find the words that would be worthy of him and the occasion. I wanted to honor my father by giving the kind of speech he would have given, but I also longed to express what was in my heart. Since I knew the experience of writing and delivering this speech would be a critical element in my journey to connect to him, I wanted to stay fully present to the experience in order to receive its healing effects.

Although the writing came easily, I found that preparing to deliver the speech was much more difficult. I tried several times to read the speech to Michelle, but each time I did I broke down crying, unable to finish. I knew I had to control my emotions during the speech, but I also wanted to express my true feelings to these people. I hoped that by going over the speech repeatedly I would become so comfortable with my feelings that I could control them without completely suppressing them.

When we entered the banquet hall that evening, the first thing that hit me was the size of the room and the number of people, more than 1500 Marine veterans and guests. Michelle and I were seated at the head table on a stage in front of the room. As I looked out over the sea of people, I could feel the anxiety building within me. Michelle was scheduled to speak first which increased my anxiety even more. When she stood up to speak, I could hear my blood pounding in my temples. She looked terrific in her white dress. I said a quiet prayer to my father and her uncle as the reassuring sound of Michelle's calm clear voice floated out over the audience:

> This evening marks the end of a long journey, a kind of pilgrimage during which an infant son grew well into manhood searching for some link to his unknown father who, as a very young man, was killed on Saipan.

> Although I've been a companion on the last miles of this journey, I sometimes feel like an intruder. For my loss and my story are very different. When Tony first heard of the Fourth Marine Division Association, he was very excited. I was supportive, but could not quite fully share his level of zealousness about having discovered the association. But one night I was casually reading one of your newsletters that was sent to Tony by Fred Everett.

> I was leafing through the Mail Call section, glancing at the pictures. In a caption under a photo of a group of Marines, the name DEWEY, my maiden name, jumped out at me. As I looked closer, I saw the name Raymond Dewey, and the face of one of the Marines in the photo was unmistakable. It was my uncle, my father's brother, who died from wounds on Iwo Jima.

> In that sudden moment, I felt a new sense of connectedness to Tony and a new kind of empathy for all that he had been through. And tonight I feel a sense of awe that two Marines banded together in battle would be

remembered in such a special way by two people banded together in marriage—a half century later.

I'd like to thank Jim Mackenzie for sending in that photo, and for calling me at Fred Everett's request. His words gave life to an uncle I never knew except through tales of heroism told by my family.

Then I'd like to thank all of you, the Fighting Fourth, for your bravery and heroism, and for your willingness to share both painful and sometimes even happy memories of World War II with me and Tony and others like us. You've made those loved ones we never knew real. You've provided us with new memories to treasure and to share with the next generation as we strive to keep their realness alive.

Tonight I'm here with my Uncle Bill, Ray's brother and a proud Marine from the 1st Division, and with my cousin, Charlie Crane, one of Ray's many nephews, who is also here to honor an uncle he hardly knew. I'm sure they both would like to join me in saying thank you for allowing this occasion of your 47th reunion to become such a special moment in our family's history.

Thank you.

I felt so proud of Michelle as I listened to her words. The way she spoke, what she had to say, the way she looked and carried herself, everything about her made me want to hug her and thank her for all she was to me. As we exchanged places at the podium, I kissed her and whispered, "Love you." Her composure and confidence before this large audience gave me strength. I looked out over the huge ballroom, breathed deeply and began:

Have you ever seen the movie, *Field of Dreams*? It's the story of Ray Kinsella, a young man who had a falling out with his father. After awhile the young man wanted to reconcile with his father but he didn't know how. The father died before his son could tell him he was sorry for having left him. In the movie, the young man is approaching middle age and, although his father has been dead for years, he finds himself thinking about his father and longing to see him once again.

One day as Ray is working in the cornfield, he hears an inner voice that tells him, "If you build it, he will come." At first, he does not understand the meaning of this voice, but eventually he has a vision that leads him to believe that if he builds a baseball field, Shoeless Joe Jackson, a baseball legend and his father's hero, will get to come back to the field and play baseball again. Although the idea sounds crazy, Ray Kinsella goes ahead and builds the baseball field. At the time, he does not realize it's actually his father who will come to the field and play ball again. In effect, the inner voice is telling him, "If you do the work you are meant to do, your father will come to you."

In the final scene of the movie, the father magically appears on the base-ball field and the son asks, "Dad, wanna have a catch?" The movie ends with Ray Kinsella and his father having a catch in the middle of the field that Ray had built.

For me, this movie shows us the power of memory and love to connect us to those we have lost through death.

My father died when I was two months old. I never saw my father and he never saw me. But for as long as I can remember, I've always imag-ined what it would feel like to finally see and talk to my father.

Throughout my life I have dealt with his loss in a variety of ways and I thought the pain of his absence was fairly well healed. But when I saw that final scene in the movie it was as though a torrent of feelings opened up inside of me and all the love we had for each other and the pain of not being able to share that love in this life came rushing out. The movie touched me so deeply that I rewound the videotape and watched it all over again. Again, the same thing happened. I knew there was something here for me. Something or someone was speaking to me inside my heart.

Over the years, my mother, Palma, was very open with me in sharing her memories of my father. But her loss was so painful that she stayed in touch with only a couple of people with whom she and my father lived when he was stationed at Camp Pendleton. But even those con-tacts were usually limited to a card or a letter at Christmas time. I was never even aware that your association existed and that you have been meeting with one another during all these years. I never imagined that I could get in touch with men who knew and remembered my father.

Love grows through remembrance and gratitude. In gratitude I want to share with you what I will always remember about this journey to find my father.

I then recounted how I first learned of their association and proceeded to review each of my contacts with the men of the Fighting Fourth, mentioning by name and personally thanking each person who had taken the time to speak with me or write to me. Then I concluded:

All of these memories have put flesh and blood into the image of the man who has been with me throughout my life.

I stand here this evening to tell you that the hurt and pain of this child has been healed through your memory and your fidelity to your fallen comrades. Michelle and I are here to thank you not only for ourselves and our families, but also for your children and the children of all the other men who served with you and are no longer with us. We appreciate and honor the sacrifices you made for us and our country and we are especially grateful for the way you have remembered and honored your fallen buddies. Over the years, by remembering those who have gone before us into that eternal peace, you have created a sacred time and place in which this world and the next are united through bonds of loyalty, fellowship, and love.

In these annual reunions you have honored those who have gone before us to that final landing beach where there is no longer any pain, or suffering, or fear, to that landing beach which will finally bring us all home—home to those we love.

All these years, I thought I was trying to find my father. But during this past year as I have listened to you who served with him and as I have looked into your eyes and hearts, I have come to know and understand that all the while my father was also trying to find me. He's been trying to show me the kind of man he was, what he valued, what he believed in, and how he loved his country and the Marines, his family and friends, my mother and me.

Last year I celebrated the anniversary of my father's death by visiting his grave with my mother and my father's two sisters, Mary and Sister Loretta. My father now lies buried on a hillside in the Catskill Mountains of upstate New York near the farm where he was raised. I placed a single red rose on his grave for all the Marines who served with him. Later, I said to Michelle, "Next year I want to observe the 50th anniversary of his death by going to Saipan."

This Wednesday, June 15, is the 50th anniversary and I won't be in Saipan because I chose instead to be here with you. Tonight, because of you, my father's presence is as real to me as if we were having a catch together as Ray and his father did in that final scene of *Field of Dreams*.

This is where my father is. This is where his spirit and the spirits of all those fallen Marines still live—in our memories, in our hearts, in our promise to be always faithful. Semper Fidelis. And, thank you.

All during the speech I struggled to maintain my composure. Just as I began, the servers started clearing away the dinner dishes. It was a bit disconcerting trying to speak over the noise of 1500 dinner settings being collected, but the distracting sound of the dishes forced me to concentrate on what I was saying. As I focused on the words, I found myself being pulled more deeply into the emotions underlying them. At times, it felt as though a deluge of emotion was about to come gushing forth, but just as my feelings reached a cresting point, breathing deeply and with a slight cracking of my voice, I eased back into control. At the end of the speech, I pulled myself together so I could express as clearly and as sincerely as possible what I felt inside.

As I concluded and thanked the audience, they began to stand and applaud. Their response, so completely unexpected by me and so obviously spontaneous for them, hit me like a clear, warm wave rising up and washing over me, bathing my spirit in a sea of affirmation and affection. Seasoned Marines and their wives, with tears in their eyes, came forward to greet Michelle and me. We could not have asked for a clearer indication that our words had honored both the living and the dead.

I never anticipated their response would be so strong. By following the pathway of my own healing, I seemed to have touched a truth that we all shared in our hearts. The intensity of the energy that filled the room confirmed my words—that my father and the other deceased Marines were truly present in our midst. It was as though the blessed souls of all those fallen heroes stood up and said, "We are here! This is where we live!"

The experience reminded me of a passage in *Black Elk Speaks*. Referring to the unknown burial place of the great warrior Crazy Horse, Black Elk says, "It does not matter where his body lies, for it is grass, but where his spirit is, it will be good to be."[5] Here in this gathering of aging warriors, young men who had lived to become fathers, grandfathers and great-grandfathers, I experienced the presence of my father's spirit and the goodness of the life I received from him.

When I looked back over the sequence of events leading up to and culminating in this evening, I gradually came to see that my journey with the Fourth Marines had placed me at a window between time and eternity, between this world and the next. At times, when I looked at my father's picture or sensed his presence, I felt as though I was in this world looking into eternity. At other times, when I talked with people who knew my father and I felt his words and spirit moving in and through me, it was as though I were in the other world looking into this one. I could feel how my father feels when he hears his friends talking about him, realizing how he is still loved and respected after all these years. Although it is difficult to find words to describe this inner awareness, I know I am not alone in experiencing the closeness of these two worlds.

Two days after the reunion in Norfolk, Carl Dearborn wrote to me:

From table #80, at the back wall, through teared eyes, I would have sworn a young Lieutenant was addressing the assembly at the Fourth Division Banquet. Not only your father but a lot of good Marines were there at that banquet. They were not in human form but all of us could feel their presence and know they were close by. By now, you know what a fine man your father was and the respect and esteem we feel for him. Be sure his story is not lost or forgotten. He died too young to be able to accomplish all that you can accomplish for him. If, as happens to me, you feel like someone is looking over your shoulder and helping you write, don't stop writing, don't even look to the rear. Someone is there, and even though your eyes don't see them, your heart does.

Chuck Landmesser was unable to attend the reunion so I sent him a copy of my talk. He wrote back: "Tony, I can't begin to tell you how much your address impressed me. Don't know if we get to smile in the next world but if we do you can bet that Lt. A.T. Moore USMC has a big smile on his face! He'd be damn proud of you."

Several months after the Norfolk reunion, I called Burke Dixon to ask some further questions about the men in my father's platoon. Burke told me that one of them, "Tinkering" John McLean, survived the war to become a jewelry manufacturer. About ten years after the war, McLean sent Burke a set of cuff links and a tie clasp that he had designed as a gift for all his Marine Corps buddies. The jewelry pattern is a gold square with a round ruby in the middle. On the ruby is a gold "4" and on the horizontal bar of the "4" are four diamond chips representing each of the four battles.

When Burke first told me this story it caught my attention, but I did not fully understand why. It was only later that I realized how the precious gems and metal of the jewelry highlighted the value of the symbol. The mandala logo of the Fighting Fourth was there from the beginning of my pilgrimage at the Quantico memorial and in every significant event thereafter. The logo of the Fourth Marines was present on the newsletter in which Michelle discovered her uncle's photograph, on the stationery of the Marines who wrote to me, in floral arrangements at reunions, and on the baseball caps and T-shirts of the veterans who told me stories about my father. The presence of the mandala symbol marked the symbolic value of my journey at every step along the way. Here was the mandala again, fashioned in rubies, diamonds and gold, to underline the precious value of the symbol. The mandala logo told me that my external journey with the Fighting Fourth was a symbolic pilgrimage, a journey to wholeness that brought me closer to my father and my own deeper self.

As I reflected back over the progress of this long journey, the words of Anchises when he embraced Aeneas came back to console me: "Oh my son, you have come at last, long expected. Oh how have I trembled for you as I have watched your career!" Then recalling how I would sit and gaze at my father's photograph whenever I became stuck or confused about how to proceed, Aeneas' response to his father welled up inside me: "Oh father! Your image was always before me to guide and guard me." I realized then that my father had always been present, fathering and loving me all along the journey of my life.

5   Journey's End

Coming Home

My external journey to find my father reached a climax at the Norfolk reunion. At first, I thought the external journey might continue with a trip to Saipan. I had often imagined going to Saipan to stand on the very spot where he was killed. At the moment of his death, a fracture line ran down through the depths of my psyche. I thought visiting the site of his death might help to heal some of that fracture. To be physically present with him in that moment, to kneel and to pray with him on the beach where he died, would comfort my soul. But whenever an opportunity to go to Saipan presented itself, I never seemed to be able to follow through. An unexplainable reluctance always intervened to prevent my going. Gradually, I came to realize that it was simply not the proper time for such a pilgrimage. Maybe at some future time I will actually go to Saipan, but at that point I accepted my reluctance as a sign that I should leave the external path and return to the inner journey. Like Ray Kinsella returning to the baseball field after his trip to Boston and Chisolm, I would conclude my journey of healing by returning to the inner realm of symbolic action. I would try to join my father on Saipan through the inner work of writing.

I began the inner work by gathering accounts, photographs, and maps of the battle of Saipan. I traced in detail the movements of my father's company during the landing on the island and located on a map the actual area of the beach where he tried to dig in the night he was killed. I even viewed movie footage of the battle assembled by the son of another Saipan veteran, but I had difficulty becoming engaged in the project. Contrary to my expectations, I did not feel drawn to follow the battle for Saipan beyond the first night. Instead, I felt pulled backward in time to the earlier battle for Roi-Namur.

Roi-Namur was my father's first experience of combat and it was the only battle he survived to its end. Although the island of Roi-Namur was smaller than Saipan and the battle for Roi-Namur lasted only two days, my father was present for the whole event. On Saipan, he was killed within hours of landing. The battle for Saipan went on for more than a month, but most of the battle was not a part of my father's story.

I decided to follow my inclination to focus on Roi-Namur. Once again, I started by analyzing maps and photographs of Roi-Namur, trying to see the scene as my father would have seen it, to experience what he might have experienced. Although I hoped that the recorded facts of the battle would stimulate my imagination, I doubted whether Roi-Namur would contribute much to my search for my father. As far as I knew, nothing significant happened to my father on Roi-Namur. I was also reluctant to spend a lot of time studying a battle that lasted only two days. Then, in the middle of one of my circular, mandala walks around my neighborhood, a very gentle voice came to me quite unexpectedly, saying, "Just be with me." That was all I heard. It was not dramatic, but it was clear. It was like the "still small voice" that had initiated my inner journey. I understood the voice to mean that my father simply wanted me to be with him for a few days of his life and to enter into his experience as well as I could.

So I returned to the materials I had collected on Roi-Namur—official published accounts, personal reminiscences of other Marines, and conversations I had with men who served with my father. A few days later, again while walking, I received another message, telling me, "Relive the history." As I reflected on my attention to the maps and photographs of the physical place and my efforts to relive the history of the events, I realized that I was being invited to follow an inner path closely resembling the one I had followed for sixteen years on my annual Jesuit retreats. The path was a method of contemplation that St. Ignatius Loyola outlined in his *Spiritual Exercises*.

The Spiritual Exercises are imaginative exercises similar to Jung's method of active imagination. At the beginning of each meditation, Ignatius directs the retreatant to make three preludes in preparation for the exercise:

> First Prelude. This will consist in calling to mind the history of the subject I have to contemplate. (102)
> Second Prelude. This is a mental representation of the place. (103)
> Third Prelude. This is to ask for what I desire. (104)[1]

These exercises had become an essential part of my inner life during my years as a Jesuit. Now, they emerged from within to guide me once again on a journey of healing. It felt like Ignatius and Jung, my two mentors, were coming together to assist me in this final phase of my journey.

So trusting the "still small voice" as an invitation coming from my father and depending on the guidance of Ignatius and Jung, I returned to the inner work of writing. To create a structure for telling my father's story, I would weave together Ignatius' method of meditation with Jung's approach to symbols and active imagination.

I began with Ignatius' Second Prelude, the mental representation of place, because it seemed to be calling for my attention. Ignatius says, "I will remain quietly meditating upon the point in which I have found what I desire, without any eagerness to go on till I have been satisfied"(76). When I was studying the maps and photographs of Roi-Namur, I felt like I was being drawn into the scene, so I decided to stay with the exercise until I was satisfied. I sensed there was some special meaning in the place just waiting to be discovered.

I turned to Ignatius for guidance on how to work with the maps and photographs to develop a mental representation of place. Ignatius' mental representation of place is sometimes referred to as the "composition of place." It is an exercise in which one composes the place in imagination by picturing its various elements. In the first exercise of the first week of the Spiritual Exercises, Ignatius offers the following directions to guide the retreatant in making the composition of place:

> Attention must be called to the following point. When the contemplation or meditation is on something visible, for example, when we contemplate Christ our Lord, the representation will consist in seeing in imagination the material place where the object is that we wish to contemplate. I said the material place, for example, the temple, or the mountain where Jesus or His Mother is, according to the subject matter of the contemplation. (47)

In subsequent exercises of the following four weeks of the Spirtual Exercises, Ignatius offers additional descriptions of the composition of place:

> ...see the great extent of the surface of the earth, inhabited by so many different peoples, and especially see the house and room of our Lady in the city of Nazareth in the province of Galilee. (103)
>
> ...see in imagination the way from Nazareth to Bethlehem. Consider its length, its breadth; whether level, or through valleys and over hills. Observe also the place or cave where Christ is born; whether big or little; whether high or low; and how it is arranged. (112)
>
> ...consider the way from Bethany to Jerusalem, whether narrow or broad, whether level, etc.; also the place of the Supper, whether great or small, whether of this or that appearance. (192)
>
> ... consider the way from Mt. Sion to the Valley of Josaphat, likewise the garden, its breadth, its length, and appearance. (202)
>
> ...see the arrangement of the holy sepulcher and the place or house of our Lady. I will note its different parts, and also her room, her oratory, etc. (220)

Ignatius guides the retreatant through the story of Christ's life, continually focusing one's attention on the physical place in which the events occur and inviting one to freely and imaginatively fill in the details. He encourages the retreatant to imagine in detail the contours of the terrain, the pathway from one place to another, the size and shape of structures, and the arrangement and appearance of the space. By imagining the physical details of the scene, one enters into a concrete experience of the event.

Using Ignatius' composition of place as a model, I immersed myself in the details of the geography and physical landscape of Roi-Namur.[2] Roi and Namur are two small islands located on the northeast corner of the Kwajalein Atoll, a triangular-shaped string of eighty-eight coral reefs and islands enclosing a calm lagoon in the midst of the surging Pacific Ocean. The Kwajalein Atoll is one of thirty-two island groups (atolls) and 867 coral reefs that comprise the Marshall Islands, covering 400,000 square miles of the Pacific Ocean 4000 miles from the coast of California. The highest elevation on the Kwajalein Atoll is thirty-three feet above sea level.

The lagoon of the Kwajalein Atoll stretches sixty-five miles southeast to northwest and eighteen miles across. Within the lagoon there is no surf. When I asked Chuck Landmesser about Roi-Namur, he said, "The water was like a lake." Outside the lagoon, heavy swells tumble and crash against the shore.

A narrow 400-yard strip of sand joins together the islands of Roi and Namur. Between the two islands, there is also a narrow 600-yard sand spit shaped like a human figure. Roi is three-quarters of a square mile and Namur is one-half square mile in size.

In 1944, Roi was covered by a military airfield laid out in the shape of a "4." Namur housed the garrison for the 3000 Japanese troops who maintained and defended the airfield. Before the battle began, Namur was covered with palm trees, breadfruit trees, and shrubs. In a photograph taken two months before the battle, I could clearly see the white beaches and the garrison buildings arranged neatly among the palm trees.

Although Roi and Namur—so small and so far from the mainland of the United States—may have seemed insignificant in terms of real estate, they were important to the war against Japan. The airfield on Roi and the atoll's large lagoon offered critical staging areas for the advance of American forces across the Pacific toward the home islands of Japan. But it was not the military significance of the islands that caught my attention and stimulated my imagination. As I contemplated the physical characteristics of the place, the images began to emerge as symbols representing the significance of the place for my father's story.

Here was a peaceful lagoon carved out of the raging ocean—a contained, safe space surrounded by uncontrollable, oceanic forces. The ocean was a familiar symbol for the unconscious. The peaceful lagoon therefore represented a protected area within which the stormy waters of the unconscious were calmed. Just as Ray Kinsella's baseball field provided a protective place within which to engage the unconscious, the lagoon symbolized a safe haven within which the turbulent waters of the unconscious could be navigated more successfully in one's journey to wholeness. Just as the raging ocean waters flowed into the lagoon and were stilled, so too the turbulence of the unconscious was calmed within the protective inner space created by the practice of active imagination and mandala symbolism.

When I applied the symbols to my father's story, I began to reflect on the significance of the composition of place. Could this place, the Kwajalein Atoll, and this event, the battle for Roi-Namur, mark a turning point in my father's journey to wholeness? Could this be the place and the conflict where his soul was made ready for the final battle of Saipan and death? As I pondered these questions, I remembered a poem by the Jesuit poet, Gerard Manley Hopkins.

Heaven-Haven

A nun takes the veil

I have desired to go
Where springs not fail,
To fields where flies no sharp and sided hail
And a few lilies blow.

And I have asked to be
Where no storms come,
Where the green swell is in the havens dumb,
And out of the swing of the sea.[3]

Hopkins compares a nun's entering the cloistered life of the convent to a sailor's entering a safe harbor after a stormy journey. The purpose of a cloistered life is to prefigure and prepare for the heavenly life hereafter, a life of spiritual union with God and with all of God's creation. Hopkins' description of the "Heaven-Haven" was so similar to the image of the Kwajalein lagoon—"Where the green swell is in the havens dumb, and out of the swing of the sea"—that I came to understand my father's participation in the battle of Roi-Namur as his preparation to enter into heavenly life. The Kwajalein Atoll was the place where my father's soul prepared to enter into its "Heaven-Haven."

I found the symbolism of the lagoon so rich and relevant that I turned enthusiastically to other elements of the composition of place. With Jung's help, I let the symbols of Roi and Namur speak to me.

Roi was the French word for king and *Namu*r was one of the titles of the Queen of Heaven (Notre Dame de Namur). The two islets were joined together by a narrow strip of land symbolizing their union. For Jung, this union of a "King" and "Queen" would represent the sacred marriage (*hieros gamos*) of the archetypes of King and Queen (*Rex* and *Regina*).[4] The "royal marriage"[5] of King and Queen was a mythological idea symbolizing the union of conscious and unconscious, the goal of individuation. The image of King (Roi) and Queen (Namur) enthroned together atop a triangular pyramid of islands was therefore a symbol of wholeness resulting from a process of psychic transformation and integration. Furthermore, the King (Roi) was crowned with a "4" (the pattern of the airfield), a quaternity that also symbolized wholeness. Finally, between the King and Queen stood a smaller figure (the narrow sand spit shaped like a human figure) symbolizing the child born of the royal marriage, the inner or spiritual man, a symbol for the deeper self.[6]

When I allowed the symbols to speak their truth, they told me that Roi-Namur was the place where my father underwent the kind of psychic transformation that gave birth to an inner integrity, a sense of wholeness rooted in the deeper self. The meaning of the place was "illuminated" by the archetypal symbolism contained in the name and the physical arrangement of the place.

Even the battle fought between the Marines and the Japanese repeated and supported this symbolic theme. The war between the two opposing sides could be interpreted as a conflict of opposites symbolizing the inner process of psychic transformation. In describing the process of transformation resulting from the conflict of opposites, Jung made the following observation:

> The warring elements of primeval chaos are unleashed, as though they had never been subjugated. . . . If the ego does not interfere with its irritating rationality, the opposites, just because they are in conflict, will gradually draw together and what looked like death and destruction will settle down into a latent state of concord, suitably expressed by the symbol of pregnancy. In consequence the king, the previous dominant of consciousness, is transformed into a real and workable whole, whereas before he had only pretended to wholeness.[7]

When interpreted as an image of the conflict of opposites, the outer conflict between the Marines and the Japanese became a symbol for an inner process of transformation. In the battle of Roi-Namur, my father encountered the primitive psychic forces of terror, violence, and hatred unleashed by war. The chaotic inner forces released by the horror of war did not overwhelm him because he allowed himself to be guided by the deeper self. Combat became a school of the heart in which his deeper self learned to navigate the unconscious forces that threatened to destroy the integrity of his soul. Because he found his spiritual center, he was able to withstand the destructive psychic forces unleashed by war. Roi-Namur was my father's mandala, a psychic container (marked with a "4") within which the conflicting elements of the unconscious could interact and become integrated.

Seeing the conflict of war as an image for the process of psychic transformation transmuted and elevated the conflict into a symbol of integration, namely, the conjunction or union of opposites (*coincidentia oppositorum*) that symbolized the mystery of wholeness[8] (*Mysterium Coniunctionis*) and the divine nature of the self.[9] The final outcome of both the interior and exterior struggles was a true, rather than pretended, integrity of soul. Chaos, destruction, and death were transformed into new life (the symbol of pregnancy), the child born of the union of opposites.

When I combined Jung's symbolism with Ignatius' composition of place, I was simply amazed at the flood of associations that came bubbling up from my unconscious. The spontaneity and energy with which the symbols emerged confirmed my belief that the battle of Roi-Namur played a special role in my father's journey to wholeness. My father's soul was being prepared for the final act of individuation, the moment of death. Roi-Namur was where the preparation took place, where he moved toward the inner wholeness he carried into eternity.

The symbolism of Roi-Namur also nurtured my hope that new life could emerge from death and destruction. Although the "warring elements of primeval chaos" were unleashed on the battlefields of Roi-Namur and Saipan, death was not the final word. I was confident that new life could emerge from this story, but I was not sure how.

Thinking about my father's soul preparing for death on Roi-Namur reminded me of something Thomas Merton wrote only days before his death. This Trappist monk, who spent twenty-seven years seeking God in monastic solitude, made a rare journey away from his monastery to participate in a dialogue between Eastern and Western monks. On December 2, 1968, Merton visited the carved figures of the Buddha at Polonnaruwa, Ceylon. Two days later, he wrote in his journal:

> Looking at these figures I was suddenly, almost forcibly, jerked clean out of the habitual, half-tied vision of things, and an inner clearness, clarity, as if exploding from the rocks themselves, became evident and obvious…Surely, with Mahabalipuram and Polonnaruwa my Asian pilgrimage has come clear and purified itself. I mean, I know and have seen what I was obscurely looking for. I don't know what else remains but I have now seen and have pierced through the surface and have got beyond the shadow and the disguise.[10]

For Merton, it was the end of his earthly pilgrimage. Six days later, on December 10, he died suddenly from accidental electrocution by a floor fan. Having finally found what he was looking for, he was ready to depart.

Merton's words consoled me with the thought that my father was also being readied for his passing to another life. Piercing through the shadow and the disguise, he found what he had been seeking through the brief span of his life. On Roi-Namur, my father saw with an inner clarity the meaning of his life. Intuitively, I knew that the fulfillment he experienced came not from some mystical vision but from the love he felt for his family and friends, my mother and me. Although only twenty-three years old, he reached a completion that made his death, although tragic, nevertheless filled with meaning. His brief but fully realized life called back a phrase I used to pray on the feast days of the Jesuit saints who died young: "In a short time, he reached the fullness of a long career." The connection with the young Jesuit saints added further meaning to my father's life and death.

My efforts to follow Ignatius' directions on the composition of place yielded such a rich harvest of images and symbols that it inspired me to step back to the First Prelude, "calling to mind the history of the subject I have to contemplate." Having composed the place in my imagination and having discovered its deeper meaning, I would now focus on the historical events.

As I began to collect the historical details of the battle, I discovered a passage in Natalie Goldberg's *Writing Down the Bones* that clarified a further purpose for my writing: "We have lived; our moments are important. This is what it is to be a writer: to be the carrier of details that make up history…Recording the details of our lives is a stance against bombs with their mass ability to kill."[11] I was a "carrier of details." By writing down the details of my father's story, I was helping my father and those who died with him to take a stand against the bombs that killed them. My work was a response to their plea for remembrance: "We have lived; our moments are important." Aware of their presence and inspired by their sacrifice, I called to mind the history of the events.

On January 13, 1944, the Fourth Marine Division sailed out of San Diego harbor bound for an undisclosed destination.[12] It was the only military division in World War II to be sent directly into combat from the continental United States. On January 17, my father, a farm boy from the rolling hills of upstate New York, celebrated his 23rd birthday on board a troop ship in the middle of the Pacific Ocean. I have no record of his thoughts at that time, but I can hear his voice and discern his spirit in the reminiscences of a fellow officer serving in the same battalion:

> The best time of day was after evening chow, for then I would go up to the boat deck with one of the other officers. Up there we would lean on the rail and look out over the ocean, watching the ever changing pattern of the convoy as it steamed along with the "cans" (Navy destroyers) and flat-tops (aircraft carriers) hovering protectively. As we stood there the sun would set in an awe-inspiring kaleidoscope of color, beauty and magnificence. I remember the indescribable vastness of the Pacific night with its far distant stars and the dark bulks of the convoy weaving silently yet purposively through the silver-sprinkled water.[13]

On January 21, the convoy arrived off the coast of the Hawaiian Islands. After a day of practice landings on Maui, the convoy headed west, bound for the Marshall Islands. Early on the morning of January 31, they arrived off the coast of the Kwajalein Atoll. They had been at sea for seventeen days.

My father's regiment, the 24th Marines, transferred from troop ships to landing ships and moved inside the lagoon, a mile or so from the intended targets of Roi and Namur. Artillery companies landed on the neighboring islands to prepare for the next day's battle. All day and night Navy ships and planes bombed the two small islands to make the landing safer for the Marines. From the decks of their landing ships, the Marines had a ringside view of the fireworks and a fore-taste of the shattering impact of battle. Because of the constant bombardment and the anticipation of battle, no one got much sleep during the night.

As the morning of February 1 approached, Roi and Namur were scarcely visible under the pall of smoke and dust created by heavy bombardment from the artillery on neighboring islands. My father's company was scheduled to board their landing vehicles at 8:30 a.m., but there was a shortage of boats. The land-ing vehicles had been used the day before to land the artillery companies on the neighboring islands. Many boats failed to return to their mother ship. Some boats were permanently lost and others ran out of gas. The assault was delayed until sufficient landing vehicles could be assembled.

At 11:00 a.m., my father and his men finally boarded a landing vehicle and headed for the line of departure, less than a mile off shore. At 11:30 a.m., they left the line of departure and headed for land. It was a thirty-minute run to the beach.

In an aerial photograph taken from the northern seaward side of Namur, I could see the landing craft 1000 yards out in the lagoon streaming in toward Namur's beaches. Puffs of smoke from naval and artillery fire drifted westward across the island. Beach Green 1, where my father's unit would land, was bare-ly visible through the smoke. He was in one of those boats churning toward the shore. I tried to enter my father's thoughts as he headed into his first experience of combat—my father, Lt. Anthony Moore of the 24th Regiment, Fourth Marine Division, I Company.

In the boat, Lt. Moore could smell the engine fumes and the salt water splashing over the side. The armored landing vehicle (LVT) in which he was riding was twenty-one feet in length and nine feet in width, just large enough to hold about twenty-five men standing up loaded with equipment. He leaned against the cold hard steel of the LVT. The walls were shoulder high. When the time came for them to land, he would have to pull himself up and over the wall and drop six feet into a cou-ple of feet of water. He had done it many times before, but there was always the chance that he would lose his footing and wind up on his back in the water, trapped like a flipped-over turtle by the weight of a waterlogged backpack.

He looked at the faces of his men. He could see they were frightened, but he knew they would do a good job. Some of them had been with him from his first days at Camp Pendleton. His men expected him to know what to do. Even when he was not so sure himself, they needed him to look sure. He was an ordinary guy just like them. That was what they admired and loved about him. But he also instilled confidence in them. They felt secure under his direction. They trusted him not to do some-thing stupid, especially something that might needlessly endanger their lives.

As he looked at Burke Dixon's round boyish face, he tried to give him a reassuring smile. He recognized and valued the warm rapport they had developed over the months of training and living together. The bond of respect and affection between him and his men was what he enjoyed most about being an officer.

Charlie Eaton's eyes sparkled as he laughed nervously. He was full of life, but he was also scared. They all tried not to show their fear, not so much to put on a good show in front of each other—they knew each other too well to be fooled by any phony gestures—but rather out of concern and respect for each other. Keeping their fear contained was the best way to support one another in a situation that might easily turn into a hell on earth.

"Tinker" McLean was already seasick. Although he was great to have around for fixing weapons or anything else that broke, he was completely disabled by amphibious landings. He could get seasick in a tub of water. He was eager to get to the beach no matter what awaited them.

Luigi Groccia was silent for a change. Usually, the other men could not get him to shut up. Perhaps he was thinking of his family back in Brooklyn. Luigi was proud of the Marine Corps emblem and bulldog he had tattooed on his shoulder.[14]

Francis Gill looked calm but distant, as though he were somewhere else.

Crowe, Erie, Ingoe, Lyman, Collins, Hagan, Haggerty, Milazzo, Palmer, Pigott, Volkert, and Jones: these were the faces and personalities he had come to know so well over the past year. They were his responsibility. They had come to depend on each other. He prayed that God would keep them all safe.

Artillery and naval gunfire continued to pound the beaches as they approached in the small craft. Although the water was calm, the shell shocks rocked their insides. Lt. Moore wanted to be ready when they hit the beach. He tried to focus on what he had learned, the kind of circumstances they might encounter and the series of tasks he had to complete. In his mind, he rehearsed the sequence of actions. First, he had to check on his men to make sure they all made it ashore. Then, he had to spread them out along the beach to minimize their vulnerability to enemy fire.

When he finally hit the water, he would be running on automatic pilot. This was his last chance to think—and to pray. He believed God would watch over him. He had been given so much, a wonderful family, a wife who fulfilled his every dream, and now a child on the way. God wouldn't take all this away from him. Or would He? Was it time to pay his dues for the full life he had been given? They all knew that many would not be coming back. The lieutenants understood that their casualties would be especially high. But he had chosen this path and he was proud of it. He was actually a little ashamed that he was so excited by the anticipation of battle. Finally, he and his men would have a chance to kick some ass and show what they had trained to do.

At 12:00 noon, the landing vehicles carrying I Company ground ashore on Beach Green 1. The scene was not what they had expected. Namur had been a palm-covered garrison of administration buildings, barracks and concrete fortifications, but the intensive pre-invasion bombing had completely leveled everything in sight. It was all but impossible to move through the mass of rubble. Most of the palm trees were torn out of the ground by their roots. The trees that were still standing had their tops blown away and looked like giant, broken matchsticks rising out of the smoking landscape.

I Company landed on a 200-yard wide strip of beach on Namur with an L-shaped pier on their right and the water separating them from Roi on their left. As soon as they landed, they headed directly inland. Their goal was to move northward in a 200-300-yard wide corridor that ran parallel to the west coast of Namur. Their first objective was a roadway (code-named Sycamore Boulevard) that ran east to west across the island. The roadway continued westward over a causeway linking the garrison on Namur to the airfield on Roi. I Company attacked directly forward, meeting enemy fire coming from pillboxes and shell holes. "The Japanese defenders were punch-drunk from the constant hammering they had received from naval, artillery, and air bombardments and were unable to put up an organized or coordinated defense. Resistance was a matter of small groups of defenders armed only with light weapons and the ingrained will to resist."[15]

The Marines advanced faster than they had anticipated. Their forward movement was hampered more by the wreckage from the bombing than by the efforts of the enemy. Within an hour they covered a quarter mile, half the distance to their initial goal.

Then at 1:05 p.m., a huge explosion rocked the island, covering the Marines with falling debris and acrid smelling smoke. Chunks of concrete, some several feet in circumference, rained down on the exposed Marines. No one in I Company was injured, but the men of Companies E and F were not so lucky. Only later would Lt. Moore and his men learn the tragic details of what had happened.

Several hundred yards to the right of I Company, two assault teams had simultaneously approached a massive, ten-foot-high blockhouse. Lt. Joseph LoPrete from Brooklyn led a platoon from E Company. Lt. Saul Stein from

Jamaica, Queens headed the team from F Company. Both men were in my father's unit during officer training at Quantico, Virginia. Following the usual procedures, someone from F Company placed a charge against the side of the blockhouse, blowing a hole in the wall. Immediately, a group of Japanese soldiers fled the building, realizing what was about to happen. Unknown to the Marines, the building was loaded with torpedo warheads. When the unsuspecting Marines threw several satchel charges into the hole in the wall, the building "vanished in an unforgettable roar."[16] Lt. Saul Stein and nineteen others were killed. Another hundred men were wounded by the blast.

All that was left of the building was a hole—ten feet deep and nearly an acre across—that immediately filled with water. Because Namur was a shallow coral island, the ocean rushed in quickly to reclaim its territory. For me, this peculiar physical phenomenon became a symbol for the psychological ordeal confronting my father and his men. The ocean waters rising to challenge the fragile stability of the coral island symbolized the power of unconscious forces surging upward from the stress of warfare and threatening the delicate balance necessary to maintain a solid island of ego-consciousness. The image seemed to warn that, in the circumstances of war, the integrity of a man's soul was as much at risk as the life of his body.

After the explosion, I Company continued to pick their way carefully through the tangle of destroyed buildings and fallen trees, hindered only briefly by occasional snipers who were quickly eliminated. By 2:00 p.m., only two hours after landing on the beach, the men reached the initial objective of Sycamore Boulevard. Some members of I Company had actually passed beyond the destination point, but they were forced to pull back because friendly naval gunfire continued to fall on the unsecured forward positions. Lt. Moore's weapons platoon of machine guns and 60mm mortars was in position along Sycamore Boulevard and "firing to the front at any target that looked the slightest bit suspicious."[17]

Lt. Benjamin Preston from Charleston, West Virginia, another of his classmates from officer candidate school, was in command of the assault platoon farthest to the left. When he spotted some Japanese hiding in a trench in front of him, he requested 60mm mortar support in order to move against them. As Lt. Moore's mortar team provided support, Lt. Preston led his men into the trench. At first all went well. The trench ran roughly perpendicular to Sycamore Boulevard. By firing machine guns directly into the length of the trench the Marines quickly killed ten or fifteen Japanese soldiers. But about a hundred yards from where Lt. Preston entered, the trench angled sharply to the right. Lt. Preston moved forward, leading his men. When he reached the unexpected right angle, he ran into eight or ten Japanese who were as surprised by him as he was by them. Lt. Preston killed four or five Japanese before he himself was killed.

What were my father's thoughts later when he saw his friend's body lying on top of his foes? My father and Ben Preston had lived and trained together from the beginning of their Marine Corps careers. Ben Preston was the first of his classmates whose death my father experienced so closely. He had tried to support his friend with machine gun and mortar fire, but it was not enough to protect him from death. Did the reality and personal loss of war come home to him as he looked down on his fallen friend? Ben Preston's picture was right next to my father's in the 24th Marines' yearbook. As I looked at their young but determined faces staring back at me and reflected on the parallel tracks of their Marine Corps careers, my heart struggled to understand my father's reaction to the death of his friend. Did he have any premonitions of his own death as he looked down on his friend and remembered how much they had shared over the previous fifteen months of living and working together?

I Company remained in position along Sycamore Boulevard for a couple of hours. During the time they spent sitting along Sycamore Boulevard they had time to reflect and lose some of their edge. The initial surge of adrenaline that carried them from the beach began to wear off. At 4:30 p.m., they were ordered to move forward, but they made little progress. So as night fell, Colonel Franklin Hart, the Regimental Commander, ordered the 24th Marines to dig in for the night and to hold the ground they had gained. It was 7:30 p.m.

Burke Dixon recalled seeing my father late in the day moving among his men as he passed the word to set up a protective perimeter. I Company had advanced about 175 yards beyond Sycamore Boulevard.

Lt. Moore placed his machine gun squad along the forward line of advance and the mortar squads farther to the rear in order to take advantage of the mortars' vertical trajectory. Since the forward line of I Company was only 125 yards from the northern end of the island at Nora Point, a very steep trajectory was necessary to keep the mortars from overshooting the island and dropping their shells in the water on the other side. The firing table for the 60mm mortar provided the appropriate angle of elevation for various distances but the shortest distance on the table was 200 yards. The firing table was therefore completely useless at 125 yards so he had to estimate the approximate angle of elevation for his mortar teams. Not being sure whether his weapons were properly targeted added to the tension of the night. Lt. Moore didn't like that kind of imprecision. So, in the anxious musings of the night, he resolved to correct the frustrating deficiency the first chance he had. If he ever managed to get off this island alive, he would calculate the exact angles of elevation for distances shorter than 200 yards.

During the night it rained two or three times. The Marines crawled under their ponchos to keep dry. Naval gunfire shelled the Japanese-held area in front of the Marines. Shells illuminated the forward area almost like daylight.

As I pictured the scene, I wondered what other thoughts might have touched my father's soul during that long night on Namur. He had spent his first day in battle and had seen death take the lives of many, friends and foes alike. The reality and imminence of death had come home to him as never before. Not knowing what tomorrow might bring, he tried to focus on what was most important, most real for him. Later, he told Chuck Landmesser that during the night he heard a Japanese soldier ringing a bell. It may have been just a warning bell, but it was significant enough for my father to mention it to his friend. The ringing bell was also significant enough for Chuck to remember my father's comment and share it with me fifty years later. I felt as though my father wanted me to attend to the sound of this ringing bell. "For one who has ears to hear," the bell contained a message that waited to be deciphered.

I wondered what the sound of a ringing bell might have symbolized for a Japanese soldier. It could have brought to mind the bells ringing during the Shinto New Year ceremony when the tolling of bells symbolizes a release from human frailty and sin: "With each peal of the temple bell, people are supposed to let go of their jealousy, anger, selfishness and 105 other vices, until a year's worth of mortal frailty fades away with the last dying vibrations."[18]

A Buddhist soldier might have heard the ringing bell as a summons to waken the true Buddha nature within. In Japanese Buddhism, the bell is a summons to full consciousness, to awareness of the Buddha nature in all of us. The bell is therefore a centering device, calling hearers back to their inner core and their true, divine nature.[19] Thus, Japanese soldiers preparing for death may have heard the tolling bell as a call to let go of a lifetime of human frailty and to be aware of their divine, inner core. Could my father have discerned a similar message in the tolling of the bell as he faced the possibility of death? Might this have been a sacramental moment in his own spiritual journey? Was the sound of the bell the call of the self to inner wholeness?

Although I could never be sure of my father's actual thoughts on that dark, rainy night, it comforts me to think of Japanese and American soldiers—separated by only a few yards of sand but divided by the insurmountable barrier of warfare and hatred—each in his own way doing his inner work, preparing his soul for the final transition to another realm. Once again, I recalled Thomas Merton gazing upon the carved Buddhas of Polonnaruwa, only days before his death, remarking, "I don't know what else remains but I have now seen and have pierced through the surface and have got beyond the shadow and the disguise."[20] Did my father's encounter with death on Namur help him to move beyond the shadow and the disguise to his true, inner self? Just in asking the question, I knew the answer was "Yes," not only for my father but also for me. Clearly, dealing with his death was an essential part of my moving "beyond the shadow and the disguise" to my true self.

As I Company waited out the long, terrifying night, some of the men heard screams they believed belonged to an American; they could do nothing. Morning rolled in and the Marines moved forward. They discovered the body of Cpl. Francis Gill, a squad leader in Lt. Moore's weapons platoon. As the sun was setting the previous evening, Cpl. Gill had unwittingly crossed the Marines' forward line and fallen into the hands of the Japanese. I Company found him with barbed wire wrapped around his head. The Japanese had placed a stick through the barbed wire and twisted it until the wire crushed his skull.

In the 24th Marines yearbook, Corporal Gill's handsome square-boned face sported a thin moustache and a cocky arch in his right eyebrow. As I looked at his photograph in the yearbook, I paused to honor this man's "crowning with thorns" and I prayed that his participation in the Way of the Cross had opened a pathway for him to a new and better life. I prayed too with my father and wondered whether he was moved to similar thoughts as he looked upon the tortured body of one of the men entrusted to his care.

At dawn, I Company was surprised by a Banzai attack. Fifty screaming Japanese soldiers rushed directly toward the Marines over the hundred yards that separated them. The Marines immediately returned fire. Although some of the Japanese managed to get within yards of the Marine positions, the Banzai attack was eventually repulsed.

At 9:00 a.m., I Company was ordered to move forward supported by a couple of tanks. Encountering little resistance, they reached their assigned destination on the northern shore of the island by 11:00 a.m. For I Company the battle for Namur was over. At 2:18 p.m. the entire island was officially declared secured. It took less than a day and a half to capture the island, but in that short time the young Marines had become combat veterans, with all the positive and negative experiences implied in that term.

The following morning, when the Marines retraced their steps over the ground they had covered on the two previous days, they witnessed the devastation of war. Thousands of dead and decaying Japanese soldiers lay in silent testimony to the irreversible destruction of war. The Marines would not have wasted much pity on the Japanese soldiers who had threatened their own lives and killed many of their friends. Nevertheless, the horror of the battle and its aftermath would shape their spirits forevermore.

Some of my father's men and fellow officers would survive more than two more months of gruesome combat in the battles for Saipan, Tinian, and Iwo Jima, and many like my father would eventually be killed, but Roi-Namur marked their first encounter with the reality of war.

It is not for me to say what other men might learn from such an experience, but I believe that as my father marched back across the ground he had fought so hard to take, the sight of so much death and destruction touched his heart in such a way that, no matter what happened later, he would never again be the same. [21] There is a darkness in the human soul that finds a suitable home in war. It is a darkness that each of us carries potentially in our hearts. Thankfully, only some of us experience its actuality. To be truly whole, one must somehow come to terms with that darkness. On Roi-Namur, I believe, my father looked into the face of darkness and the light in his soul was not overcome. When the time came for him to die four and a half months later on Saipan, the light in his soul entered peacefully into the Light from which it had come.

After the battle for Roi-Namur, the Marines returned to Maui in the Hawaiian Islands to rest and train for their next engagement. On Easter Sunday, 1944, Lt. Moore took Burke Dixon out to the firing range to practice firing the 60mm mortar. During the night on Roi-Namur, the proximity of the Japanese and the inadequacy of the firing table had made it impossible to get an accurate aim on the enemy. Having to guess at the correct setting in such life-threatening circumstances was completely unacceptable to the lieutenant. In the terror of the night, he had decided that he would one day determine the precise mortar set-tings for ranges of less than 200 yards.

Lt. Moore and Burke Dixon spent the afternoon of Easter Sunday firing a mortar and calculating the appropriate angle of elevation for dis-tances of 100, 125, 150, and 175 yards. The lieutenant then wrote the corresponding ranges and settings in blue ink at the top of the firing table.

Several weeks after the Norfolk Reunion, Burke Dixon sent me the firing table on which my father had recorded the ranges and settings. He had been sav-ing the firing table since the end of the war and wanted me to have it as a memen-to. The old cardboard chart was yellowed and creased from being folded in four and stuffed into a shirt pocket or wallet, but the numbers, written in blue ink, were clearly legible.

As I held the firing table in my hand and looked at the numbers written by my father's hand, I could feel his sense of accomplishment in finally remedying a situation that had caused him so much worry and concern in combat. His men would now be better equipped for whatever circumstances confronted them in subsequent battles. Little could my father have foreseen that the firing table would survive the war and, decades later, be held by his son. Holding the card-board he once held, I lamented that we never held each other.

When Burke told me that he and my father calculated the mortar settings on Easter Sunday, I figured my birthday must have been around the same time, but

I did not realize how close it was until I consulted an almanac. In 1944, Easter Sunday fell on April 9. I was born one week later on April 16, the First Sunday after Easter. April 9 is as close as I can get to determining what my father was doing when I was born. The date brings my father's life closer to mine and gives me a fixed point to connect his life to mine. Easter Sunday afternoon, April 9, 1944, provides a link between my father's life and my birth, thereby lessening my sense of separation and disconnection.

As I reflected on the consolation I felt in learning this date, I realized that much of my inner wound came from the close connection between my birth and my father's death. I was especially troubled because his death followed so quickly after my birth. At some strange unconscious level, I almost felt that my birth had caused his death, that the world could not hold the two of us alive at the same time. There seemed to be a deadly inevitability in the temporal sequence of April 16 and June 15, the dates respectively of my birth and my father's death, an inevitability that held me captive. Somehow, learning about Easter Sunday, April 9 released me from the deadly pattern of a death following immediately after a birth.

The new date, April 9, opened the possibility of an alternative temporal sequence, April 9 and April 16, a sequence that suggested a different pattern of meaning: two Sundays bracketing the First Week of Easter. Instead of associating my birth (April 16) with my father's death (June 15), I could now link my birth with a day in my father's life (April 9), an Easter Sunday celebrating our birth to new life in Christ's Resurrection. By joining our two lives together at the beginning and end of Easter Week, the dates of April 9 and April 16 provided a life-giving sequence to counterbalance the deadly sequence of April 16 and June 15.

Learning what my father was doing on April 9 changed my attitude toward my own birth. Previously, I had viewed my birth as the prelude to my father's death. Now, I could relate my birth to a week in my father's life and, more importantly, a week that celebrated the mystery of the resurrection of the dead. The liturgical readings for the First Week of Easter narrate the various ways the Risen One appeared to his friends after his death. In a marvelously personal way, I now experienced the power of the Resurrection in coming to know my father, truly and intimately, years after his death.

Moreover, the symbolism of the two Sundays bracketing the First Week of Easter focused my attention on the meaning of the liturgical seasons. Easter is the central feast of the Christian liturgical year, a ritual calendar of seasons that transforms secular time into sacred time by recapitulating the story of Christ's life, death and resurrection. The firing table that I held in my hand became a tangible symbol, a sacrament, that my father's life and mine were united in sacred time, a time that transcends the limitations of secular time. Although my father and I never met in physical time, we met symbolically in sacred time, the First Week of Easter. By recapitulating the story of the final months of my father's

journey to wholeness, I entered into sacred time where my own journey of healing came to a close.

In an article Chuck Landmesser sent me, I found a perfect liturgical image
to complete my father's journey to wholeness. Chuck had written the article for
Leatherneck magazine in 1949. The article began, "There never was, and there
never will be, another Christmas Eve like that Christmas Eve of 1944 in the camp
of the Twenty-fourth Regiment of the Fourth Marine Division on the island of
Maui."[22]

It was the first Christmas after my father's death. The Marines who survived
the battles for Saipan and Tinian were back on Maui with a batch of fresh recruits
training for their last and most gruesome battle, Iwo Jima. Chuck painted a vivid
picture of the scene as the Catholic Marines gathered for Midnight Mass and
were joined by many of their non-Catholic buddies. Dressed in ponchos and helmet liners, the Marines streamed out of their tents and headed toward the outdoor
theater where an altar had been constructed from 37mm ammo boxes and covered with a white target cloth. The nostalgic sound of Christmas hymns played
over the padre's loudspeaker system, reminding everyone of home and
Christmasses past.

Chuck shared his own thoughts and feelings as he and the other survivors
gathered in prayer and remembrance:

> The moon hadn't risen but the stars of Hawaii glittered brightly as the
> chaplain talked of home and dear ones. You leaned forward on your
> sandbag, chin in hand, and listened. As he spoke, your thoughts turned
> again to Christmas at home, but soon you were thinking about your bud-
> dies who were present at Mass last Christmas, but who had since fallen
> on the white sands of the Marshalls, on the rocky ledges of Saipan and
> Tinian.

> You wondered how many of those sitting around you tonight would be
> missing from the next Midnight Mass. The thought that you yourself
> might not be present next year made you pray earnestly and drink in the
> loveliness and sublimity of the scene. You said a prayer for Soapy, Sam
> and Tony, wondering if they were hovering near.

When I read Chuck's words, I was moved by his prayerful remembrance of my
father and two other buddies at Mass. The ghostly presence of the fallen Marines
"hovering near" caught my imagination. I could see my father and the other
Marines standing around the priest at the altar made of ammo boxes, looking
down lovingly on their friends and praying with them.

The image of my father at the altar reminded me of a story my mother used
to tell about going to Mass with my father in a small California town. When the
priest came out of the sacristy to begin Mass, he had no altar server. In those
days, the presence of an altar server was considered an important element in the
rubrics of the Mass. The ritual was somehow less solemn without an altar serv-

er. When my father saw that the priest had no altar server, he left my mother's side and joined the priest at the altar to be his server. My father was dressed in his Marine uniform.

The image of my father dressed in a Marine uniform and standing next to the priest at the altar of sacrifice was the way I imagined him on that first Christmas Eve following his death. The sacrifice of his life was united with the sacrifice of the altar. The image epitomized my belief that on the beaches of Roi-Namur and Saipan my father achieved a kind of wholeness and holiness that he carried into eternity. For me, the image was a confirming symbol that in the end my father came home to his "Heaven-Haven," "where flies no sharp and sided hail and a few lilies blow."

By following Ignatius' first two preludes (the composition of place and recounting the history), I had discovered a rich treasure of concrete details and symbols in my father's journey to wholeness. As I became more engaged in his story, I also began to experience the positive effect that writing his story was having on my own journey of healing. The parallel process between my father's journey to wholeness and my own journey released a welcome flow of healing energy from the deeper levels of my unconscious. Ignatius' Third Prelude—"ask for what you desire"—offered me an opportunity to reflect more specifically on the impact of my father's story on my own healing process.

When I began my research on the battle of Roi-Namur, I was conscious of a desire to know my father more intimately and to heal whatever required healing at this stage of my journey. But it was only as I worked my way through the composition of place and the history of the battle that I began to appreciate the precise content of my desire. While I was writing the story of Roi-Namur, the symbolic imagery surfaced so quickly and generated so much energy within me that I realized the battle of Roi-Namur was important not only to my father's story but also for my own inner work. Jung said "a dearly loved father"[23] might sometimes appear in dreams as a symbol for the self. What I learned through the symbolic action of writing was that the image of my father served as a symbol for the deeper self guiding my inner work. By entering concretely into my father's experience on Roi-Namur, I was engaged in my own journey to wholeness. Eventually, I came to understand that my father's request for me to be with him was in effect a call from the deeper self inviting me to complete my father archetype.

According to Jung, the father archetype is an empty pre-existent form that acquires specific content from one's conscious experience of fathering figures. In my conscious experience, the father archetype received content from my grandfather, uncles, priests, and other fathering figures, but it remained relatively empty with respect to my own father because I never knew him. By learning and writing about the details of my father's history, I was in effect filling in the missing content that I had not received from my own father. The integrating work of the self was achieved by consciously connecting to the father archetype and enriching its content, thereby allowing the rich psychic energy associated with the archetype to flow into conscious experience.

Telling my father's story healed the fracture that ran through my psyche at my father's death. I have now come to understand how, with simple fragments like a cardboard firing table or the sound of a ringing bell, we can weave together a pattern of meaning to heal our psychic wounds. Following the guidance of the deeper self, I have learned how to reweave the fabric of my soul and "come home" to the wholeness I lost at my father's death.

As I was finishing the writing of my father's story, I had two dreams, approximately a month apart, that confirmed for me the positive effect of this work on the unconscious level. In the first dream, the President's daughter was telling me how to enter the White House. Then, I walked into a beautiful new addition to my Aunt Rita's house. The addition was a very modern steel structure with high ceilings and lots of glass. When I entered the structure, I realized that my Aunt Rita's house had been expanded by adding many beautiful new rooms. The new rooms formed an arc around the original small wooden structure. In the second dream, my Uncle Pat's daughter led me into her father's house which was joined to the house next door by the addition of a new structure between the two original houses. Again, the expanded interior was new and beautiful.

I interpreted the dreams to mean that the anima, the sister of my soul, appearing first as the daughter of the President and then as the daughter of my father's brother, was leading the ego into a new home: a beautiful, newly expanded, psychic dwelling place. This home was associated with the king archetype (President/White House) and the father archetype (Aunt Rita = father's closest sister; Uncle Pat = father's brother and Best Man). Because of my father's death, fundamental aspects of the king and father archetypes had remained inaccessible to me. Now, the unconscious was telling me in the dream that the ego was at home in the Father's House, the House of the King—the creative and generative energies associated with the king and father archetypes were available to consciousness.

It did not require much of an intuitive leap to realize the spiritual implications of the dream for the image also described the Heavenly Kingdom:

> In my Father's house are many rooms; if it were not so, would I have told you that I go to prepare a place for you? And when I go and prepare a place for you, I will come again and will take you to myself, that where I am you may be also. (John 14:2-3)

On the beaches of Roi-Namur and Saipan, the Lord was preparing a room for my father in the Heavenly Kingdom. When his life journey ended, my father went home to his Father's House. By drawing me into the story of his life and death, I knew that my heavenly father was also preparing a room for me. Although my earthly journey was not yet over, I too was coming home.

On a conscious level, I experienced the integration of the father archetype in the energy, enthusiasm, and confidence that flowed through me as I moved closer to the final stages of this writing project. When I started out and often throughout the early and middle stages of this project, I was so filled with self-doubt and anxiety that it was nearly impossible to work for more than an hour or two each day. But as I began to connect to the energy of the father archetype, I learned to trust the inner truth of what I was doing. I became less critical and judgmental about the work, worrying less about how it would be received by others. I was more willing to accept the truth that I was writing the book that was in me and that it would be futile to try to write anything else. The reassuring message coming up from the deeper recesses of the self to calm a doubting ego was, "If you do the work you need to do, the fruit of that work will find its way into the hands of those who will benefit from it." That belief has brought to closure a project that at times I thought would never end.

6   Postlude

I began this writing project because I wanted to know my father. The process of writing and the healing that flowed from the writing gave me the courage to look into areas that previously I had hesitated to enter. I knew my mother had saved some of my father's letters, but she had always been unwilling to share them with me. She said they were too personal. She seemed to be embarrassed by the intimacy and romantic tone of the letters. "We were so young," she said, "I would not want anyone else to read them." For years, I honored my mother's wishes concerning the privacy of my father's letters, but whenever she hinted that she might destroy them, I would plead with her not to do so.

All the inner work I did with my father seemed to change my feelings about those letters. Through symbolic action and soul work, I had come to know him in a way that I never dreamed possible. Now I was ready for a more intimate encounter with him. It was almost as though my father was inviting me to read the letters in order to enter more deeply into his most intimate feelings and thoughts. So, late one Saturday afternoon while visiting my mother, I said, "Let's take a look at Dad's letters." Surprisingly, she said, "Okay."

Together, we went into her bedroom and removed the dusty boxes and papers that covered her hope chest. My mother had saved the hope chest my grandparents gave her as a wedding present. Down at the bottom of the hope chest, tucked into a corner, was a brown paper package. The package was surrounded by linen sheets that my grandmother had placed in the hope chest in preparation for the wedding. I took out the package and examined it. It was a manila envelope addressed to my mother with her maiden name. The return address was from Siena College, Loudonville, N.Y., where my parents had met as students. Inside the envelope was a thick stack of letters. As I opened the first letter and began to read, it was as though my father stepped into the room. Here was his handwriting, so similar to mine, though I had never seen it before. He was writing to my mother about the little things in his life, his hopes and dreams for the future. He was no longer speaking to me through symbols, photographs, or other people but in his own words, directly from his heart.

My mother and I had been preparing to go to 5:30 p.m. liturgy when I suggested we look for the letters. So, not wanting to be late and feeling a desire to pray, I put the letters on the kitchen table and took my mother to Mass, carrying inside me the excitement of this new discovery. It felt as though a new door was about to open through which my father would enter. Sitting next to my mother in the church where I served Mass as an altar boy and celebrated my first public Mass as a priest, I prayed in thanksgiving for all that I had already received and in anticipation of what might still lie ahead.

After the liturgy, my mother and I returned home and sat at the kitchen table, the center of our family life for seventy years. Together, we read one of the letters. In the letter, my father was telling my mother how much he loved her and that she was everything he ever wanted out of life. I think the intensity of his feelings surprised both of us. Through her tears my mother said, "Now you know why I never remarried." My tearful response was: "I'm glad we are reading these together while you are still alive. It would be a lot more painful to read these words after both of you are gone." We tried to read another letter together, but it was clear my mother had read all she could handle. So I quietly put the letters aside and began to prepare supper for us.

Only in retrospect did I recognize the symbolic overtones of what we were doing: the two of us gathered together at table remembering a loved one who had gone before us. Like the friends of Jesus after his death and like Ray and Annie Kinsella after building the baseball field, my mother and I were participating in a totem meal.

When I left my mother's and returned home, I took the letters with me. I spent the next three days reading slowly through each letter. There were seventy letters, dated from June 23, 1942 to February 2, 1943, covering the period of my parents'courtship, their preparations for marriage and a brief period after their wedding. My father began writing to my mother when he returned home to the family farm after graduation. The letters recounted his summer activities while waiting to receive his active duty starting date. During that time he worked on the farm with his brothers and visited with my mother several times, at her home and his. In late August, he left for Quantico and began his Marine Corps training. The only time he saw my mother during training was on a romantic November weekend they spent together in Washington, D.C. On January 25, 1943, they were married in my mother's parish church. After a four-day honeymoon, my father went to New River, North Carolina where the Marines were assembling the Fourth Division. He wrote the last three letters from New River while he was waiting for his new bride to join him.

As I read the thoughts and feelings he shared with my mother, I was amazed to discover how much of my father lives in me. It felt as though the core of his soul lived on in my soul. We were so much alike in the things that really mattered to us. The way he expressed his love for my mother was so similar to things I wrote to Michelle that it was almost eerie to read his words. Even his physical complaints and his worries about successfully completing the officers training program sounded exactly like me. Family members had often commented on my physical resemblance to my father. In reading the letters, I realized that the resemblance ran down to the depths of my being. His letters were like a mirror held up to my own soul. Just as I saw his freckles or the slant of his right eyelid in my own face, I recognized the deepest longings of my heart in what he wrote to my mother.

The letters made me feel like I really had a father, that there was a particular person who not only gave me physical life but also influenced my spiritual and psychological makeup. I had noted the similarities between us when I first heard his fellow Marines talking about him, but in the letters he revealed himself directly to me without any intermediaries. He was telling me who he was at the very center of his being. I could actually feel myself receiving essential elements of my own soul from my father. It was a more intense experience of the ancient Indian belief that a dying father's secret vitality and personality are carried over into the life of the son. I never realized how much I had longed for this gift until I actually received it.

Furthermore, when I reflected on the content of my father's letters, I realized the reciprocal nature of our relationship. I was not the only one to benefit from our kinship. Reading about his hopes and dreams for the future—dreams that had appeared to die on the beach of Saipan—I saw clearly that the heart of those dreams had come true in my own life. I have been privileged and blessed to live the life he had dreamed of living. I could hear my father echoing the words John Kinsella spoke after playing baseball on the field his son had built: "For me, it's like a dream come true." I trust that my father too experiences his dreams coming true in the life I lead and the work I do.

Now as I look into my father's eyes in a photograph, I feel that I really know him and that I am really known by him. We know each other from the inside. The letters tell me: if I ever want to be with my father, all I have to do is look deeply into my own soul, into the deepest longings of my heart. And whenever I feel disconnected from my own soul, I need only be with him for awhile to find my way again.

■ ■ ■

My father's body came home when I was four years old.
His soul joined mine as I told his story and wrote this book.

Notes

CHAPTER 1

[1] C. G. Jung. *Collected Works* (Princeton University Press), Volume XVIII, par. 398.

CHAPTER 2

[1] D. D. Groff. *Kansas City Star*. September 30, 1990. *Field of Dreams* was filmed on a baseball diamond carved from a cornfield near Dyersville, Iowa. Since the film's release, thousands of pilgrims have traveled each year from around the world to visit and play on the field the moviemakers left behind. Many people have sent me articles or told me stories describing the powerful attraction and enduring fascination of that Iowa field for a variety of pilgrims.

[2] Jung makes a distinction within the psyche between consciousness and the unconscious. Consciousness refers to those thoughts, memories, and feelings that are present in one's awareness. The unconscious constitutes the mysterious reservoir out of which consciousness emerges. "In childhood [consciousness] awakens gradually, and all through life it wakes each morning out of the depths of sleep from an unconscious condition." C.G. Jung. *Collected Works* (Princeton University Press), Volume XI, par. 935.

[3] The ego is the center of conscious life. The ego is gradually shaped by the various roles *(personae)* one assumes in adapting to the outer world.

[4] Within the unconscious, Jung distinguishes the collective unconscious from the personal unconscious. The personal unconscious contains material derived from the life history of the individual. The collective unconscious is derived from the common history of the human race. The archetypes are pre-existent forms rooted in the collective unconscious. The father archetype is a universal, primordial image that relates to male parenting figures.

[5] The self is the archetype of psychic wholeness, a primordial image that integrates the conscious and unconscious dimensions of psychic life, thus expressing the unity of the personality as a whole. The self is the center of the totality of psychic life, including both conscious and unconscious. "The self is not only the center but also the whole circumference which embraces both conscious and unconscious; it is the center of this totality, just as the ego is the center of consciousness." Jung. *C.W.*, XII, par. 44.

[6] Jung divides the individuation process (i.e., the movement toward psychic wholeness) into two phases, corresponding to the two halves of life. The goal of the first half of life is to establish a strong ego identity. The goal of the second half of life is to allow the deeper self to emerge as the center of the totality of psychic life. Mid-life transition marks the shift from the first phase to the second phase of the individuation process.

[7] Jung. *C.W.*, V, xxvi.

[8] Jung. *C.W.*, IX, i, par. 533.

[9] Jung. *C.W.*, IX, i, par. 558.

[10] Jung. *C.W.*, XIII, par. 325.

[11] Jung. *C.W.*, IX, i, pars. 235-6.

[12] Clarissa Pinkola Estes. *Women Who Run With The Wolves*, (New York: Ballantine Books, 1992), p. 52.

[13] For Jung, a mandala is a universal symbol of the self that expresses the psyche's orientation toward wholeness. Mandalas are "geometrical structures containing elements of the circle and quaternity; namely, circular and spherical forms on the one hand, which can be represented either purely geometrically or as objects; and, on the other hand, quadratic figures divided into four or in the form of a cross"(Jung. *C.W.*, IX, ii, par. 351). Radial arrangements, i.e., figures formed by radii emanating from a central point, are also mandalas. A baseball field is a mandala because it is a radial arrangement with two foul lines radiating from home plate, defining a circular arc in the outfield, and containing a four sided figure, the diamond.

[14] Active imagination is a conscious engagement with images that arise spontaneously from the unconscious. By engaging these images through activities such as writing, drawing, dancing, or working with physical materials like stone or wood, we allow them to reveal their symbolic meaning and thereby open consciousness to the psychic energy associated with these images.

[15] C.G. Jung, *Letters*, (Princeton, N.J.:Princeton University Press, 1973),Vol. I, p. 416.

[16] Jung. *C.W.*, XI, par. 339.

[17] "From the beginning I felt the Tower as in some way a place of maturation—a maternal womb or a maternal figure in which I could become what I was, what I am and will be. It gave me a feeling as if I were being reborn in stone. It is thus a concretization of the individuation process." C.G. Jung. *Memories, Dreams, Reflections*, ed. Aniela Jaffe (New York: Random House, Vintage Books, 1965), p. 225.

[18] Jung. *Memories, Dreams, Reflections,* pp. 173-5.

[19] Jung. *C.W.*, XVIII, pp. 171-2.

[20] The collective unconscious is rooted in the common inheritance of humankind. Jung postulated the existence of the collective unconscious based on the evidence that certain common themes and patterns appear in the myths and stories of many cultures, even cultures that had no direct historical influence on each other. The common themes and patterns that arise from the collective unconscious Jung called archetypes. "The concept of archetype . . . is derived from the repeated observation that the myths and fairytales of world literature contain definite motifs which crop up everywhere. We meet these same motifs in the fantasies, dreams, deliria, and delusions of individuals living today." Jung. *C.W.*, X, par. 847.

[21] The anima/animus archetype is an inner personification, opposite in gender to the conscious personality. Within the unconscious, the distinction between the sexes symbolizes the contrast between conscious and unconscious. Since a man's outer, conscious personality is predominantly masculine, his inner unconscious life is represented by female figures. In the case of women, it is just the opposite: a male figure represents the inner unconscious life. Jung chose the Latin feminine word, *anima*, for a man's inner feminine figure and the Latin masculine word, *animus*, for a woman's inner masculine figure.

The primary function of the anima/animus is to serve as a bridge between the collective unconscious and conscious life, introducing archetypal figures to the ego and facilitating communication between the ego and the collective unconscious. Anima and animus are inner personalities that mediate the depths of the unconscious to the individual and assist in connecting the conscious ego to the unknown world of the unconscious. See John Welch. *Spiritual Pilgrims,* (New York: Paulist Press, 1982), pp. 167-170.

[22] Jung. *C.W.*, XIII, par. 62.

[23] Jung. *C.W.*, XI, par. 242.

[24] Jung. *C.W.*, IX, i, par. 242.

[25] Jung. *C.W.*, XIV, par. 128.

[26] Jung. *C.W.*, XI, par. 157.

[27] Jung. *C.W.*, XI, par. 156.

[28] Edward F. Edinger. *Ego and Archetype*, (New York: Penguin Books, 1973), p. 96.

[29] Jung. *C.W.*, VIII, pp. 419-531. Jung developed the concept of synchronicity to account for certain psychic parallelisms that could not be explained by the principle of causality, e.g., two people having the same dream. Such synchronous events led Jung to postulate that there are connections at the unconscious level that go beyond the cause and effect relations that characterize conscious life. These connections seem to depend on activating archetypal processes in the unconscious. That is to say, when one moves down to the deeper, shared level of the collective unconscious, one gains access to certain processes which are common to all people and not limited by the confines of one's unique conscious personality.

[30] John Welch. *Spiritual Pilgrims*, (New York: Paulist Press, 1982), p. 37.

[31] "The figure of the wise old man can appear...not only in dreams but also in visionary meditation (or what we call 'active imagination')...The wise old man appears in dreams in the guise of a magician, doctor, priest, teacher, professor, grandfather, or any other person possessing authority. The archetype...appears in a situation where insight, understanding, good advice, determination, planning, etc., are needed but cannot be mustered on one's own resources. The old man thus represents knowledge, reflection, insight, wisdom, cleverness, and intuition on the one hand, and on the other, moral qualities such as goodwill and readiness to help." Jung. *C.W.*, IX, i, par. 398.

[32] Jung. *C.W.*, XII, par. 159.

[33] The poet Robert Bly discovered the same phenomenon in his work with men who were psychologically derailed by the deaths of the Kennedys and Martin Luther King: "Many men of the generation now forty-five or so projected their undeveloped inner King on Jack Kennedy, who spoke openly of Camelot, and on Martin Luther King, and on Bobby Kennedy. When forces in the United States opposed to any spiritual kingship killed the Kennedys and King in mid-career, it was a catastrophe for the men of that generation. Some men have told me in tears that they lost something then, and have never regained it; they have never gotten back on track." Robert Bly. *Iron John*, (Reading, Mass.: Addison-Wesley, 1990), p. 111.

[34] Robert A. Johnson. *Inner Work*, (San Francisco: Harper & Row, 1986), p. 61.

[35] Jung. *C.W.*, XI, par. 149.

[36] "Every archetypal image carries at least a partial aspect of the Self. In the unconscious there is no separation of different things. Everything merges with everything else. Thus, as long as the individual is unconscious of them, the successive layers we have learned to distinguish, i.e., shadow, animus or anima, and Self, are not separated but merged in one dynamic totality. Behind a shadow or animus problem or a parent problem will lurk the dynamism of the Self. Since the Self is the central archetype, it subordinates all other archetypal dominants. It surrounds and contains them. All problems of alienation, whether it be alienation between ego and parent figures, between ego and shadow, or between ego and anima (or animus), are thus ultimately alienation between ego and Self. Although we separate these different figures for descriptive purposes, in empirical experience they are not usually separated. In all serious psychological problems we are therefore dealing basically with the question of the ego-Self relationship." Edinger. *Ego and Archetype*, pp. 38-39.

[37] "The ego-Self axis represents the vital connection between ego and Self that must be relatively intact if the ego is to survive stress and grow. This axis is the gateway or path of communication between the conscious personality and the archetypal psyche. Damage to the ego-

Self axis impairs or destroys the connection between conscious and unconscious, leading to alienation of the ego from its origin and foundation." Edinger. *Ego and Archetype*, p. 38.
[38] Jung. *Memories, Dreams, Reflections*, p. 227.
[39] "If we do our work inwardly and do small rituals to express our inner situation, it often generates a great charge of constructive energy in the external world around us and shapes our external circumstances in ways that we would never have anticipated. This is part of the evidence we have for the existence of the collective unconscious: We find that the unconscious connects us to other people and to our entire environment; therefore, when we focus a great deal of energy within the inner world, a parallel energy often arises in the people or situations around us. In this way we can do healing through our inner work that we never could have done through external means." Robert A. Johnson. *Inner Work*, p. 105.

CHAPTER 3

[1] Louis J. Puhl, S.J. (Trans.) *The Spiritual Exercises of St. Ignatius*, (Westminster, Maryland: Newman Press, 1957), # 2.
[2] Seamus Heaney, *Selected Poems: 1966-1987* (New York: Farrar, Straus and Giroux, 1990), pp. 3-4.
[3] Pierre Teilhard de Chardin. *The Making of a Mind*, (New York: Harper & Row, 1965), p. 57.
[4] Virgil. *The Aeneid*. Trans. by C. H. Sisson. (Manchester: Carcanet Press Ltd, 1986), p. 164.
[5] Virgil. *The Aeneid*, pp. 165-166.
[6] Jung. *Memories, Dreams, Reflections*, pp. 158-159.
[7] Jung. *C.W.*, XI, par. 782.

CHAPTER 4

[1] My father fought on Roi-Namur and was killed on Saipan. The battles on Tinian and Iwo Jima took place after his death.
[2] Carl Dearborn. *Marine Verses from WW II*, p. 33.
[3] Jung. *Memories, Dreams, Reflections*, pp. 77-78.
[4] Giuseppe Tucci, *The Theory and Practice of the Mandala*, Trans. Alan Houghton Brodrick, (London: Rider & Company, 1961), pp. 89-90.
[5] John G. Neihardt. *Black Elk Speaks: Being the Life Story of a Holy Man of the Oglala Sioux*, (Lincoln: University of Nebraska Press, 1961), p. 145.

CHAPTER 5

[1] Louis J. Puhl, S.J. (Trans.) *The Spiritual Exercises of St. Ignatius*, (Westminster, Maryland: Newman Press, 1957).
[2] Details of the geography and landscape of Roi-Namur are taken from Robert D. Heinl and John A Crown, *The Marshalls: Increasing the Tempo*, (Washington, D.C.: U.S. Marine Corps Historical Branch, 1954).
[3] W.H. Gardner & N.H. MacKenzie, *The Poems of Gerard Manley Hopkins*, (Oxford: Oxford University Press, Fourth Edition, 1970), p. 19.
[4] Jung. *C.W.*, XIV, pp. 258 ff.
[5] Jung. *C.W.*, XIV, par. 541.
[6] Jung. *C.W.*, XIII, par. 118.
[7] Jung. *C.W.*, XIV, par. 506.
[8] Jung. *C.W.*, XVI, par. 537.

[9] Jung. *C.W.*, XIV, par. 176.

[10] Thomas Merton, *The Asian Journal of Thomas Merton*, (New York: New Directions, 1968), pp. 233-236.

[11] Natalie Goldberg, *Writing Down the Bones*, (Boston: Shambhala, 1986), p. 44.

[12] Details of the Battle of Roi-Namur are taken from Robert D. Heinl and John A. Crown, *The Marshalls: Increasing the Tempo*, (Washington, D.C.: U.S. Marine Corps Historical Branch, 1954) and Albert Arsenault, *Personal Account*.

[13] John C. Chapin, *Personal History of Camp Pendleton, Namur, Saipan and Tinian*.

[14] Later, on Saipan, Luigi Groccia was wounded in his tattooed shoulder. When he stood up to shake his fist at the Japanese for messing up his tattoo, he was shot through the neck and killed. Burke Dixon was kneeling at his side.

[15] Heinl and Crown. *The Marshalls*, p. 88.

[16] Heinl and Crown. *The Marshalls*, p. 90.

[17] Albert Arsenault. *Personal Account*, p. 22.

[18] M. Jordan and K. Sullivan. "A New Year for Reflection: Japanese Gently Hail Holiday at Holy Shrines." The Washington Post, January 2, 1996.

[19] When a Catholic priest asked Thich Nhat Hanh how to practice mindfulness, the Zen Buddhist monk answered, "Use your bell as a bell of mindfulness, calling you back to your true home." Thich Nhat Hanh, *Living Buddha, Living Christ*, (New York: Riverhead Books, 1995), p. 23.

[20] Thomas Merton. *The Asian Journal of Thomas Merton*. (New York: New Directions, 1968), p. 236.

[21] Another mortar platoon Marine reflecting on his first combat experience expressed a sentiment that I believe my father would have shared. He wrote, "As I crawled out of the abyss of combat, I realized that compassion for the sufferings of others is a burden to those who have it. …[T]hose who feel most for others suffer most in war." E.B.Sledge. *With the Old Breed at Peleliu and Okinawa*, (Novato, California: Presidio Press, 1981), p. 158.

[22] C.A. Landmesser. "Christmas Eve on Maui." *Leatherneck: Magazine of the Marines, December*, 1949, pp. 19-20.

[23] Jung. *C.W.*, IX, ii, par. 354.

Bibliography

Books

Bly, Robert. *Iron John*. Reading, Massachusetts: Addison-Wesley, 1990.

Edinger, Edward F. *Ego and Archetype*. New York: Penguin Books, 1973.

Estes, Clarissa Pinkola. *Women Who Run with the Wolves*. New York: Ballantine Books, 1992.

Goldberg, Natalie. *Writing Down the Bones*. Boston: Shambhala, 1986.

Hanh, Thich Nhat. *Living Buddha, Living Christ*. New York: Riverhead Books, 1995.

Heaney, Seamus. *Selected Poems: 1966-1987*. New York: Farrar, Straus & Giroux, 1990.

Heinl, Robert D. and Crown, John A. *The Marshalls: Increasing the Tempo*. Washington, D. C.: U. S. Marine Corps Historical Branch, 1954.

Hopkins, Gerard Manley. *The Poems of Gerard Manley Hopkins*. Edited by W. H. Gardner and N. H. MacKenzie. Oxford: Oxford University Press, 1970.

Johnson, Robert A. *Inner Work*. San Francisco: Harper & Row, 1986.

Jung, C. G. *Collected Works*. Translated by R. F. C. Hull. Edited by Sir Herbert Read et al. 20 Vols. Bollingen Series XX. Princeton, N. J.: Princeton University Press, 1953-1979.

——. *Letters*. Vol. 1: 1906-1950. Princeton, N. J.: Princeton University Press, 1973.

——. *Memories, Dream, Reflections*. Edited by Aniela Jaffe. New York: Random House, Vintage Books, 1965.

Loyola, Ignatius. *The Spiritual Exercises of St. Ignatius*. Translated by Louis J. Puhl, S.J. Westminster, Maryland: Newman Press, 1957.

Merton, Thomas. *The Asian Journal of Thomas Merton*. New York: New Directions, 1968.

Neihardt, John G. *Black Elk Speaks: Being the Life Story of a Holy Man of the Oglala Sioux*. Lincoln: University of Nebraska Press, 1961.

Sledge, E. B. *With the Old Breed at Peleliu and Okinawa*. Novato, California: Presidio Press, 1981.

Teilhard de Chardin, Pierre. *The Making of a Mind*. New York: Harper & Row, 1965.

Tucci, Giuseppe. *The Theory and Practice of the Mandala*. Translated by Alan Houghton Brodrick. London: Rider & Company, 1961.

Virgil. *The Aeneid*. Translated by C. H. Sisson. Manchester: Carcanet Press, 1986.

Welch, John. *Spiritual Pilgrims: Carl Jung and Teresa of Avila*. New York: Paulist Press, 1982.

Film

Field of Dreams. Written for the screen and directed by Phil Alden Robinson. Universal City Studios, 1989.